AWAKEN YOUR
AUTHENTIC LEADERSHIP

AUTHENTICITY JOURNAL

"Authentic Leadership training, which included completing the Authentic You™ Personal Planning System, introduced us to a completely new way of approaching our working environment, with tools to become more self-aware, to connect more deeply with our values, and to integrate this knowledge into our leadership. Learning as a small group, we had an experience much like holding hands at the side of a pool and jumping in together at the same time – it was a risk worth taking, with refreshing results that are visible in my leadership approach on a day-to-day basis.

The training is a must for leaders seeking to create productive, motivated, emotionally mature, and supported teams. It reminds us all "how to be" as successful leaders in a modern, relevant workforce."

Sally Thorpe

"The Authenticity Journal supports the PPS (Authentic You™ Personal Planning System) by providing a space for us to collect our thoughts and reflections, and is a reference for us as we move forward. It provides a touchstone that we can reference, see where we've been, and often surprise ourselves at how much we've grown. The journal also supports the Authentic Leadership book, and I've noticed even the most reluctant writers are motivated to record their questions, learnings, and reflections as a way to document the process of personal groundwork through Tana's guided system."

Jenn Wicks, Coach

"Working through the Personal Planning System helped me clarify and articulate the challenge I was identifying in my work environment as well as the tension I felt between my work reality and my personal values and goals. From there, with coaching support, I was able to explore an inspiring direction forward and formulate my next steps. I was able to make a radical career transition in a gradual way that honored my deepest values, strengthened my relationships, and allowed me to continue to address some of the workplace challenges I was leaving behind."

James David Thomas, Author | Coach | Facilitator

"The knowledge I gained from participating in the Authentic You Personal Planning System provided me with the ability to learn to live each day as 'me', allowing me to follow my newly discovered purpose and strive to achieve those never-before articulated goals. Above all, I began to live life with a sense of calm, knowing my life is playing out as it is meant to be. For me, the Authentic You Personal Planning System provides a doorway to infinite possibility and alignment with one's self."

Sarah Clarke, Career Development Coach

"The Personal Planning System by Tana Heminsley continues to support me through my life's journey. Its systematic approach provides me with the awareness I require to understand who I am deep within my soul, an imperative element to my leading a truly authentic life. Time after time, and in the most chaotic and difficult U-turns in my life, I turn to the PPS as it provides me with the ability to find clarity about where I am heading and what I want in my life. During times of disconnect, transition, and especially, lack of purpose and direction, I utilize this system as it offers the successive awareness I need to wake up and discover each new path along my continual personal evolution."

Diana Reyers, CEO of Daringly Mindful™, a Storyteller, Author and Human Advocate.

Other books by the Author

Awaken Your Authentic Leadership –
Lead with Inner Clarity and Purpose

Contributing Author:
Daring to Share – 8 Brave Souls Sharing their Authentic Road Trip,
by Diana Reyers

Coming soon:
Awaken Your Authentic Leadership –
Lead with Inner Clarity and Purpose (for Women Leaders),
by Tana Heminsley and Helena Demuynck

EASE – An Authentic Approach to Living your Best Life

AWAKEN YOUR AUTHENTIC LEADERSHIP

Authenticity journal

TANA HEMINSLEY

AUTHENTIC LEADERSHIP GLOBAL
PUBLISHING DIVISION

Authentic Leadership Global, Inc. – Publishing Division
#603-1328 Marinaside Cresc
Vancouver, B.C.
Canada
V6Z 3B3
tana@leadauthentic.com
www.leadauthentic.com

ISBN 978-1-7771921-0-5

*For organizational leaders who want to start now
to discover their unique and authentic way of leading and living.*

Relax into your authenticity and live this day with just a little more ease....

Walking Between

Walking between the known and the
re-discovered, re-claimed...

between the "normal" ways of being in the world

the current "truth"...

and the "new" normal.

The rock is being pulled up
slowly uncovering a different way....

Some are peaking out and testing the earth around for stability... for welcoming...

Others are searching... opening...
Making the ground ready...

Together we are walking between, and co-creating different ways....

the new normal for the world.

—Tana Heminsley,

Table of Contents

Foreword

Who has profoundly and positively influenced your life? This is a question I often ask myself and my clients. For me, one person stands above the rest. Tana Heminsley, my mentor, sponsor, colleague, friend and inspiration, is a woman who personifies and models authentic leadership in a way that motivated me to become not just her follower, but her champion.

We met nearly a decade ago, a time of significant personal and professional growth in my life, one that was profoundly influenced by Tana and her ground-breaking work on authentic leadership.

During that time, I earned two degrees at Vancouver British Columbia's Simon Fraser University (SFU), studying in leading graduate programs at universities in Brazil, Mexico and the United States. I have facilitated hundreds of managers through leadership development programs and guided coaches and facilitators around the globe through Tana's Authentic Leadership programs. Throughout this period of personal and professional development and growth, I have used Tana's Authentic You™ Personal Planning System to guide my decision-making. Understanding my own values and seeking to live into them fully, connected to my purpose and attentive to my overall wellbeing has supported me in clarifying my vision and setting and achieving my goals.

Life wasn't always like this for me. I have experienced working in a toxic organization and working with leaders who demonstrated a lack of clarity in their values and an inability to self-manage their impulses. In my personal life, I struggled for years in an unhealthy marriage. Becoming dedicated to living a life of authenticity has dramatically shifted those experiences. My work relationships are now based on aligned values; rewarding and mutually supportive. I now celebrate being in a loving, supportive marriage that is based upon shared values. My husband and I use the Personal Planning System to annually update our vision for a life that is adventurous, rewarding and also focused on doing what we can to make the world just a little bit better. Today I can truly say that I am living fully expressed in my values, aligned with my purpose, achieving goals that I couldn't have even imagined accomplishing a decade ago.

Tana and I were introduced by an acquaintance who felt that we had much in common. At the time I was facilitating leadership retreats in British Columbia, for women, as was Tana. We met and talked over tea and a walk in West Vancouver's Ambleside Park. That first conversation sparked a professional and personal relationship that over the years has deeply enriched my work and my life. In the months following that initial meeting, I attended extraordinary dinner gatherings hosted by Tana that brought together professional women to connect and have authentic conversations on a variety of topics. Before long, I was learning how to host those conversations myself, guiding leaders to connect more deeply with themselves and others. I came to appreciate that a leader is anyone who steps up and influences others. With that in mind, I began facilitating authentic conversations with groups of parents and teens, sharing with them Tana's philosophy that authentic leaders have awareness, inner clarity and a life-affirming and ethical intent.

In addition to her passion for supporting others in developing their self-awareness, emotional intelligence and wellness, Tana is a prolific producer of inspiring, transformative learning materials that are as accessible as they are compelling. This journal exemplifies that.

In addition to my own experience and those of my clients, I have enjoyed guiding clients of Authentic Leadership Global™, through the steps outlined in this journal. Witnessing participants experience the insights that have accelerated their personal and professional growth has been particularly rewarding, not only for me, but also for the facilitators and coaches who have received training and subsequently shared its wisdom and insights with their clients.

Gaining inner clarity in a world so replete with confusion and distractions is challenging. Tana's Authenticity Journal offers a pathway of ease to seeking and finding clarity. My personal experience has been that understanding my values, being able to clearly articulate my sense of purpose and then developing my vision and setting goals from that perspective energizes everything that I do. My clients who have embarked on this journey share similar feedback on their experiences. My personal experience and what I witness in others who have embarked on this journey is that we are living more fully expressed, authentic lives, caring for ourselves, one another and this planet. I think we need more of that in this world and Tana and I welcome you on the journey.

Laura Mack MBA
Certified Authentic Leadership Program Facilitator & Trainer, Authentic Leadership Global™
http://www.linkedin.com/in/livingauthentically

Introduction

Since I published my first book in 2013, *Awaken Your Authentic Leadership – Lead with Inner Clarity and Purpose,* I have been sharing it with organizational leaders, human resource professionals, coaches and facilitators around the world. In addition, individuals who did not see themselves as leaders have been reading it and are learning that they really are - as they step up and influence others by doing the right and ethical thing each day.

As I took hundreds of clients through the steps of the Authentic You™ Personal Planning System, I learned a few things that I hadn't understood when I published the first book in 2013. I'd like to share them here so you can take this updated context into your thinking as you complete the steps of the system contained within.

First, authentic leadership is important and it's becoming increasingly helpful in business. In 2015 authenticity was declared by Harvard Business Review as the "gold standard" for leadership.[1]

Second, Authenticity is about being choiceful (a word I took liberty to add to the dictionary in my first book). The process of becoming your authentic self and living aligned with what is deeply important to you, is largely about remembering and practicing intentional, inner-guided, and ethical choice.

Third, authentic leadership is supported by emotional and social intelligence. In my first book I had yet to reconcile the two and left you with the question about whether they were the same. Since then, the MHS EQ-i 2.0 Assessment Report for Emotional Intelligence helped to make it clear. In it the authors provide the following definition:

> "An authentic leader serves as a role model for moral and fair behavior. A transparent approach commands esteem and confidence from employees."[2]

It goes on to list emotional intelligence skills that are important to develop in order to be an authentic leader. A simple way to think of the two concepts is that authentic leadership takes emotional intelligence to the next level by adding in the "moral and fair" (or ethical) component.

Fourth, the Authentic You™ Personal Planning System supports strategic planning at the individual level and I've added a couple of steps that make it different from other systems. It is very flexible in how it's used – in 1:1 coaching, as a retreat for a team, as a series of conversations for team building for cross-company cohorts. It can support leaders to experience profound results – both personal and leadership transformations that they couldn't have imagined before they began the steps. With my clients' permission, I've shared some of these stories in the chapter called "What to Expect".

---

1   Bill George, The Truth about Authentic Leaders, Harvard Business Review article, July 6, 2016.

2   MHS EQ-i 2.0 Assessment Report, pg 6.

Fifth, the order that the steps are completed is important. The first step – articulating who you are as your best or authentic self, helps to overcome the lens of the inner critic to allow you to remember your potential. If you jump into the other steps first, they may be clouded by "shoulds" rather than being open to the possibilities of what could be.

Sixth, consistently clients have proven that the step to uncover their Purpose, is one where they articulate their unique way to help make the world a better place. Whether that is to leave a legacy for their children or to help others realize their full potential, articulating their Purpose sets the stage for envisioning their life dedicated to fulfilling the reason they were put on this earth. What is distinct is how this manifests for each person.

Seventh, Leadership Principles could really be called "Tactical ways to express your Purpose". Bill George, author of "True North – Discover Your Authentic Leadership" defines Leadership Principles as "A set of standards used in leading others, derived from your values. Principles are values translated into action."[3] After working with clients over the years, I found it helpful to stick with the tactical focus and to ask them questions like "If this is who you are at your best, and these are your values and Purpose, how do you want to live these each day? What are the tactical ways you want to express them? Or What don't you want, and how does that inform what you do want?" which lead to answers such as "I don't want to travel at all anymore, or I want to travel one week/month, or I want to build teams, or I don't want to manage people, or I want to work from home 1 day/week, or I want to work with people who inspire me".

Leadership Principles inform the step on clarifying your Life Vision. Once you have answered the big questions that you will explore in the first three steps (Authentic Self, Values and Purpose), Leadership Principles support you to get tactical and define clearly what that looks like on a day-to-day basis. With this as context, the Life Vision is clearer and the possibilities that emerge are often different than what the client envisioned when they began their exploration.

Eighth, it was important to have the option of either setting specific Goals or more broad statements of Intention. Many clients have had their fill of setting specific goals and wanted to put their thoughts for progress on paper without the constraints of being specific. For others, setting goals was essential as it gave them more rigor and clarity that helped to propel them forward into action. If you use Goals, add in a specific action you could take to begin to achieve it; if you use Intentions, add in something that you will pay attention to that points to achieving your Intention.

Ninth, the Inner Development Plan can be tricky to complete on your own as developing practices to create change may be a new skill to develop. Once in a while the unhelpful patterns of thought or behaviour that are getting in your way, may be unknown to you whereas others around you can see them clearly. While I've written the instructions for this step to focus on practices to improve self-awareness and self-management, the solution may require other steps. Try completing it on your own, and if you find it challenging, seek support from someone who can help - a coach, friend or your manager.

And finally, a couple of additional learnings – clients asked for more space to complete the Action Worksheets than I had provided in the foundational book. So I created the Personal Learning Journal as a handout for them that they used to document their thoughts as they completed the process. Over the years, they came back for several refreshes as their life had evolved - they had gotten a promotion, or had another child, or what they were doing had lost its meaning.

Thus the *Authenticity Journal* emerged.

---

3   Bill George, *True North – Discover your Authentic Leadership,* (San Francisco: Josey-Bass, 2007) p 87.

Awaken Your Authentic Leadership sets the context for what authentic leadership is, why it is important, the characteristics of an authentic leader, how the neuroscience works, and then provides the detailed instructions for working through each step of the Authentic You™ Personal Planning System.

The *Authenticity Journal* provides the space to do the work and have several iterations of the Personal Learning Journal in one place. This can then be used to go back to over and over again, to see the progress you have made, and to celebrate the changes that have occurred in your leadership and more broadly in your life.

Never underestimate the ripple effect you have as an authentic leader!

Tana Heminsley

What to Expect

The following are expanded versions of the testimonials provided at the front of the book as well as additional stories provided by those who have been using the Authentic You™ Personal Planning System over the years as a support system to live and lead their authentic lives.

They provide details about the kinds of insights and shifts you can expect to experience when you read and "do" the steps outlined in this book.

· · · · · · · · ·

"I purchased Tana's initial book to help my team find themselves and become authentic leaders. Authentic leadership offers great insight into how to lead by knowing yourself, who you are and where you are. Knowing your own compass bearings is essential to leading others authentically and wholeheartedly. An honest self-discovery journey that touches both personal and professional aspects of your life is key to tapping into the powerful learnings that Tana provides through her book and work. It can be viewed as EVERYTHING that is important to leadership! Every time I work with Tana's tools and processes, something new is revealed. The experience results in people resonating with people; and being authentic inspires and motivates people in a real "rubber meets the road" way – you are more effective, more aware, more proficient."

Lindsay Thompson, Director, Indigenous Relations

· · · · · · · · ·

"The Authentic You™ Personal Planning System turned my world upside down in the best possible way. It brought a clarity of self, purpose and an ability to create goals that I had never before experienced and the result of this clarity jumpstarted an unexpected and unbelievably positive evolutionary process in my life.

When the opportunity to complete the program presented itself to me, the timing was perfect; it was exactly what I needed. At 40 years old, I had been feeling a sense of turmoil or rumbling inside me for the previous couple of years regarding how I presented myself to the world and where my career was going but I had no idea how to address it.

I didn't know that 'I' (my authentic self) was hiding inside me just waiting to be let out, nor could I articulate who 'I' was. I didn't know what career I should be pursuing; I only knew that my current career wasn't what I wanted to do for the rest of my working life. I had no idea the opportunities that awaited me.

The knowledge I gained from participating in the Authentic You™ Personal Planning System provided me with the ability to learn to live each day as 'me', allowing me to follow my newly discovered purpose and strive to achieve those never-before articulated goals. To make what was happening even better, the more I lived like this the more opportunities presented themselves to me. For example, I was offered a new role in my company, created specifically for me, that is in complete alignment with my purpose and authentic self; additional learning and development opportunities that I wanted to pursue were supported by my employer and I became able to improve the relationships and deepen the connections with the people in my life. Above all, I began to live life with a sense of calm, knowing my life is playing out as it is meant to be.

For me, the Authentic You™ Personal Planning System provides a doorway to infinite possibility and alignment with one's self."

Sarah Clarke, Career Development Coach

• • • • • • • • •

"I first encountered Tana Heminsley's Authentic You™ Personal Planning System in 2013, at exactly the right time for me. Working through this system, with Tana's amazing guidance and support as a coach, gave me the clarity of purpose and commitment to embrace a time of transformation.

Before the Personal Planning System, I was searching for a new career direction and a way to move forward. After working through the Personal Planning System, I had the confidence to commit to the radical career change I was exploring and take my next steps in a purposeful and gradual way that honored my deepest values and larger commitments.

I had recently attended Harvard Business School's Program for Leadership Development and was looking to harness my background and experience in engineering and multi-discipline project management in new ways, preferably as an entrepreneur.

Over the previous five years, I had become increasingly aware of the limitations of traditional management approaches – common within engineering and construction workplaces – to consistently deliver truly amazing results. Formal processes could move projects forward in predictable ways, often with an underlying focus on managing compliance. But these approaches, based on a technical, mechanistic perspective of the world of work, typically failed to support the full authentic presence and participation of team members.

Many of the projects I was involved with meant bringing together a diverse team to focus on a project goal. The reasons for the team's existence, and for individuals to participate as part of the team, often remained pragmatic, if not transactional or contractual. Rather than everyone seeing themselves as team members with a shared purpose, contractual arrangements divided people into consultant teams, or construction teams, or client teams, or other stakeholders. Rarely were team goals discussed in a larger, more inspiring frame that could make sense of project work as progress towards shared worthwhile causes or as honoring the deeply-felt personal values of participants as members of a single team.

While reasons for team existence and member participation remained pragmatic or contractual, true collaboration and teamwork remained a surface veneer over unspoken conflicts, secret negotiations, and disguised power plays designed to advance the agendas and self-interests individual or sub-groups. What struck me was that true collaboration and teamwork would only emerge when all those involved could reframe their participation in terms of a larger meaning for belonging to a single team.

What was missing in the traditional methods and formal processes was the acknowledgement and elevation of truly relational perspectives. We would talk about engagement and collaboration in terms of planning how to make people engage and collaborate. Within traditional engineering and construction workplace cultures, we invoked a mechanistic, objectifying, and self-interested approach to work that replaced worthwhile causes and inspiring values with pragmatic goals and contractual compliance.

Without a shared language for a more relational approach, we had no chance of inviting the formation of true communities with inspiring shared purposes for moving any project forward. Without recognizing and shifting our traditional workplace cultures, we couldn't crack the code for authentic full participation or the emergence of innovative and truly amazing results.

That's where Tana's Authentic You™ Personal Planning System came to my rescue. Working through the Personal Planning System helped me clarify and articulate the challenge I was identifying in my work environment as well as the tension I felt between my work reality and my personal values and goals. From there, with coaching support, I was able to explore an inspiring direction forward and formulate my next steps. I was able to make a radical career transition in a gradual way that honored my deepest values, strengthened my relationships, and allowed me to continue to address some of the workplace challenges I was leaving behind.

With the support of coaching and the Personal Planning system, I cut a fresh path through the unknown. I transitioned from the engineering world to a new career as a leadership coach and team training facilitator, specializing in helping traditional managers and project managers explore more relational approaches to their work worlds and broader lives. I've since become a published author and continue to explore how a more relational approach to our life situations can help all of us lead more meaningful and satisfying lives at our authentic best.

Five years ago, I could hardly have imagined the fresh paths I have since discovered, made possible by the clarity the Personal Planning System brought me as I took those initial steps."

James David Thomas, Author | Coach | Facilitator
James is the author of the book series
"Unselfish: How to be a Better You in these Self-Obsessed Times."

• • • • • • • • •

"As Tana's client, I have read her book and been coached through the Authentic You™ Personal Planning System (PPS). This process has helped me to work through areas of deep personal growth, and has led to lasting change for me and people close to me. I have revisited the entire PPS several times now - for myself, as I encounter and take on new life challenges, and with my clients - both in groups and in one-to-one coaching. And each time, I learn new things about myself and how I want my life to be.

As a coach, I have led many of my clients through the Authentic You™ PPS. Like me, my clients have experienced powerful learning and personal growth as a result of completing the guided exercises, and focusing on the questions presented as well as ones they come up with. It is at once an exercise in self-discovery and a practice for continued inquiry and reflection that we seldom make time for in our busy lives. It provides us with a framework for our coaching together, and something tangible to reference when appropriate.

The Authenticity Journal supports the PPS by providing a space for us to collect our thoughts and reflections, and is a reference for us as we move forward. It provides a touchstone that we can reference, see where we've been, and often surprise ourselves at how much we've grown. The journal also supports the Authentic Leadership book, and I've noticed even the most reluctant writers are motivated to record their questions, learnings, and reflections as a way to document the process of personal groundwork through Tana's guided system.

Jenn Wicks, Coach

• • • • • • • • •

"The Personal Planning System by Tana Heminsley continues to support me through my life's journey. Its systematic approach provides me with the awareness I require to understand who I am deep within my soul, an imperative element to my leading a truly authentic life.

Time after time, and in the most chaotic and difficult U-turns in my life, I turn to the PPS as it provides me with the ability to find clarity about where I am heading and what I want in my life. During times of disconnect, transition, and especially, lack of purpose and direction, I utilize this system as it offers the successive awareness I need to wake up and discover each new path along my continual personal evolution.

As a coach, The Personal Planning System provided me with the confidence to offer an efficient tool to my clients that provided the highest degree of efficacy towards reaching their personal and professional goals. To be able to offer someone the support they are seeking to catapult them towards their life's purpose while, simultaneously, connecting them to their truth provided me with immeasurable satisfaction and gratification.

Tana Heminsley is an intuitive genius when it comes to guiding individuals towards their authenticity. The Personal Planning System reflects her innate knowledge and intention as she offers this valuable gift to the world for each of us to use. This is your personal and professional opportunity to use a proven system as you discover authenticity and move forward within it."

Diana Reyers is the CEO of Daringly Mindful™, a Storyteller, Author and Human Advocate. A retired Authenticity coach, Diana dedicates her mornings to writing her collaborative book series, Daring to Share, in conversation with ordinary individuals sharing extraordinary stories, and organizes storytelling events surrounding authenticity. Diana's book launch tour begins October 10, 2018 in Coombs, British Columbia on Vancouver Island. To connect with Diana and for more information about Daring to Share, go to daringtoshare.com

• • • • • • • • •

"Working with the Personal Planning System and my coach helped me get clear on my goals. By going through this process, I was able to put some structure in my schedule that eventually helped me achieve my goal of recording my next album. The accountability process of checking in each week kept me on track. The results were fantastic."

**Kara Grainger, Performing artist, Musician, Singer, Songwriter,
Latest album "Living with Your Ghost"
Coach: Leslie Ritter, Authentic Leadership Coach**

• • • • • • • • •

"Tana Heminsley created something special when she pulled together emerging elements of leadership, authenticity and emotional intelligence into her first book, *Awaken Your Authentic Leadership: Lead with Inner Clarity and Purpose,* based on her flagship program for leaders, coaches and facilitators – Authentic Leadership Global™. Tana's action worksheets and online journal have helped me clarify my own personal and business vision, mission and goals. My clients love them too! They connect with their purpose and authentic selves, often for the first time in their lives. The impact for my clients is life-long, as they open up their leadership and conversations to greater alignment with their purpose and most important values. This connection to authentic self allows clients to show up more fully as an authentic leader, and to build greater trust in themselves and in their professional and personal relationships.

Tana's long-awaited Authenticity Journal pulls together all the elements of the Authentic Leader's journey into one place, and is a true gift! One I can't wait to share with clients, and to use myself!"

Carrie Gallant JD
Leadership and C-IQ® Coach, Mediator and Negotiation Strategist

• • • • • • • • •

"The Personal Planning System in Tana's book has provided the clarity I needed to move toward accomplishing the goals I set out for my life and work. Following the system has brought out my vision for how I want to be and shown me how to build the path towards the life I want to be living both now and in the future. To miss out on a system like this that can serve you throughout your life, not just one time, would be to not realize your full potential and ability to contribute to the world and others in meaningful ways."

Michael Brough

• • • • • • • • •

"The Personal Planning System provided the framework to further articulate my passion and who I truly am. I developed greater self-compassion and inner strength to create boundaries so that I could remain (and return) centred. Clients were able to use the personal planning system to became confident leaders in their organizations, communities, and families - aligning the values and principles they discovered as guiding factors in their lives."

Trina Rowsell
Author | Coach | Facilitator | Mentor | Nutritional Consultant

• • • • • • • • •

"The Authentic You Personal Planning System, supported by the Authenticity Journal provides a powerful encounter with your essence. Immerse in this Journey and experience the awakening of what is truly important in your leadership and in your life. The Authenticity Journal will allow you to translate your awakening into authenticity principles and practices, enabling you to bring a new, compelling kind of Authentic Leadership into the world."

Helena Demuynck
Certified Authentic Leadership Coach | Systemic Team Coach | Conflict Coach

My wish for you

That you re-discover your authentic self, your unique path as authentic you, live authentically and intentionally, and realize your full potential....

This Authenticity Journal is for you to record glimpses of your self, your dreams, your goals and leadership principles, etc., as you build self awareness and continue your personal and leadership development....

Language is powerful—I have used the language that is meaningful for me so if something doesn't resonate, I encourage you to change the words to what is meaningful for you.

This simple system can be paired with reflection and new awareness, to refocus your leadership and life any time you feel the need... annually, during transition, or when you seek new meaning or possibilities. What you discover today may be different from another time in the future, as you evolve and grow.

How to Use the Authenticity Journal

Spending time learning about yourself through self-reflection and journaling will support you to get clear about who you are and what is important to you at this stage of your life.

This Authenticity Journal is the companion guide to the book *Awaken Your Authentic Leadership – Lead with Inner Clarity and Purpose*. The foundational book provides the context for understanding what authentic leadership is, what the qualities of an authentic leader are, what the business case is, and why authentic leadership is important. It also outlines what the Authentic You™ Personal Planning System is and provides detailed instructions and insights for each of the 10 Steps.

The *Authenticity Journal* provides the working papers for reflecting and capturing your thoughts as you work through each of the steps for the first time, as well as for 4 additional iterations.

You can use both books each year (or anytime you have a life change) to recalibrate your life and reconnect to your Inner GPS. This is then used to guide your decision making in order to make more choices that are aligned with what is deeply important to you.

Part One

The Authenticity Journal contains one sets of the following materials so that you can work through the Authentic You™ Personal Planning System in detail:

Action Worksheets – We've included the ten Action Worksheets with lots of room for you to work through them and make notes as you go. These provide simple exercises to help you see new possibilities, create new habits, and build new skills to be authentic. Think of them as the draft version of your personal discovery work, so your Inner Critic can relax just a little bit while you do.

Personal Learning Journal – These are the summary pages that you can use to transfer in the final version of the information you will uncover as you work through the Action Worksheets. You can then take photos of each page and keep it on your smartphone so you have it within reach and available for whenever you need help navigating.

Part Two

Four additional blank copies of the Personal Learning Journal have been provided so you can recalibrate your inner guidance system for four additional years and the information is all in one place. You can then reflect back to earlier iterations to see how you have evolved since you began your journey to awakening your authentic leadership with our guidance.

Part One –
First set of Action Worksheets
and Personal Learning Journal

Action Worksheets

Use the following Action Worksheets to complete each step of the Authentic You™ Personal Planning System, for the first time. Once you have completed each step, transfer the final product either into your Personal Learning Journal, or onto your Authentic You™ Poster (for those of you who like to use large-format poster-board paper to capture your learnings visually as well).

1. Remember your Authentic Self
2. Articulate your Values
3. Discover your Purpose
4. Clarify your Leadership Principles
5. Create your Life Vision
6. Assess your Work-Life Balance
7. Reflect on your Awakening and the implications for your Leadership
8. Set your Goals
9. Create your Inner Development Plan
10. Putting it into practice

Authenticity

Grounded
Heart-centered
Able to see ego in the moment
for what it is...

Old, automatic patterns
Unconsciously on autopilot
Once awakened
are seen for what they are...

Merely thoughts
passing like clouds...

When I stay present and live in the moment
Choosing the vertical life
connected to source
intelligence moves through me
the answers come...

Clarity in the moment...

Authenticity.

—Tana Heminsley

— Step #1—
Remember your Authentic Self

Use one or all of the following action worksheets to support you to remember your Authentic Self.

There is an important distinction between authentic leaders and other leaders: Authentic leaders understand that their potential is broader than what they are aware of at this moment.

Their current awareness may include aspects of themselves that have developed to this point in their lives. They may be aware of their strengths and they may also be aware of their opportunities to be more effective. They may have noticed their tendency to react too quickly, or to interpret situations incorrectly, and the impact this has had on themselves and others.

They may also be unaware of other aspects of self that are undiscovered or more accurately have been forgotten —joy, compassion, creativity as well as the ability to be clear and firm; aspects that are covered up by the layers of personality.

The distinction between parts of ourselves that we are familiar with and that may act as strengths or obstacles, and our deeper, clearer, selves that we may have covered up is referred to as personality (or ego) and Authentic Self.

> Authentic Self is who you are when at your best — a creative and compassionate person with the unique qualities that make you who you are. It is your potential and your birthright.
>
> Personality includes the aspects of self that develop from birth to adulthood as a result of influences and experiences in our lives — those that are helpful (strengths) and those that are no longer helpful (self-limiting thoughts and beliefs).

Beneath the layers of personality lives the true nature of the person—the Authentic Self —always there and waiting to be rediscovered and remembered. The number of layers of personality, particularly those that are unhelpful or unhealthy, depends on many factors including genetics, upbringing, culture and lifestyle.

> Generally, we do not experience our Essence and its many aspects because our awareness is so dominated by our personality. But as we learn to bring awareness to our personality, it becomes more transparent, and we are able to experience our Essence more directly.[4]

---

4   Don Richard Riso and Russ Hudson. *The Wisdom of the Enneagram – The Complete Guide to Psychological and Spiritual Growth for the Nine Personality Types* (New York: A Bantham Book, 1999), p 27..

Your Authentic Self shines through more often as you understand and engage your strengths, see the self-limiting thoughts and behaviours for what they are, and let them go in order to make choices aligned with who you truly are.

EXERCISES

This first exercise is an important first step, orienting your thinking to your potential for who you are when at your best.

Before beginning, center, relax and be open to the exercise you are about to complete.

Personal Research

a) Reflect on the following questions for yourself. Then ask 3 or 4 people — your family, colleagues, friends, boss and/or team — to write down their perception of you. Ask them:

- Who am I when at my best?
- What are a few words you would use to describe me when I am at my best?
- What is my gift in the world? What am I good at? What do you think I should be doing in my next chapter?

b) Write down your own reflection about yourself here. Words that describe you when at your best are:

1.

2.

3.

4.

5.

c) Write their names and responses below:

Respondent One – Name and Responses:

Respondent Two – Name and Responses:

Respondent Three – Name and Responses:

Complete one or all of the following exercises before completing your final list.

Self-reflection — Life steps/Career/Life Journey/Educational Training

Complete the following table for each job or career step you have taken to your life at this point. Include your age, the job you had at that time or the name of the position you held, whether the experience was fulfilling (+) or not (-) and 1-2 words that describe your way of being when you were most fulfilled. The first few lines provide an example:

Your age or the year (approx):	Life Steps, Job or Position, Educational Training:	Level of fulfillment you experienced during this time. Show visually with one or more of each (+) or (-):	Words to describe your way of being when you were most fulfilled:
18	Finished high school	-	Hopeful
25	Writer for a local newspaper	+++	Courageous, Curious, Empathetic
33	Got divorced	--------------	Resentful, Vengeful, Sad, Resigned

Complete a 360 Review

Complete a 360 Review with your supervisor, peers, people who report to you, friends or family. There are many different types and forms of 360 review.

a) Use the following questions to create your own simple questionnaire and feel free to adapt it in a way that feels right for you:

- What are my strengths?
- What are my opportunities for development?
- What two things do I not know about myself that would be helpful for me to know (may be blind spots for me): Positive and Negative.
- What beliefs do I have that support me to be effective?
- What beliefs do I have that may be getting in my way?
- Any other feedback for me?

b) Write the words that stand out from the responses that describe you at your best, below:

Respondent One–Name and words they used to describe me:

Respondent Two–Name and words they used to describe me:

Respondent Three – Name and words they used to describe me:

Respondent Four – Name and words they used to describe me:

Use a Personality or other Self-Assessment to understand your potential

Assessments can be helpful when completing your personal research. These can include the Riso-Hudson Enneagram Type Indicator, Myers Briggs Type Indicator Assessment (MBTI)®, Insight Inventory®, Strengthsfinder Assessment, TTI Emotional Quotient Assessment, Authentic Leadership 360 Assessment, etc. There are many more available. They can also be helpful to refer to again and again over time to develop new awareness.

a) Complete one or more personality or other self-assessments to understand your potential. Write the words that stand out in your assessment results that describe you when at your best, here:

Assessment:

Words this Assessment provided me to describe my Authentic Self:

Assessment:

Words this Assessment provided me to describe my Authentic Self:

Assessment:

Words this Assessment provided me to describe my Authentic Self:

Using the Enneagram to discover your potential

Use *The Wisdom of the Enneagram* book together with this exercise to discover your potential as Authentic Self.

Discover your preferred type

First, take one of the many free online tests available, or the complete RHETI test using the link to the Enneagram resources on the Enneagram Institute website and/or complete the test in *The Wisdom of the Enneagram* book called the QUEST (Quick Enneagram Sorting Test)[5].

Using your results, notice the Enneagram type that has the highest score (e.g. Type Three – The Achiever) — if you are here, you may have discovered your type.

If there is more than one type with a high score (e.g. you score seventeen points on each of types Three, Seven, and Eight) on your results, do the following for each:

- Using *The Wisdom of the Enneagram* book, turn to the chapter that is focused on each type. There are 15 questions for each that will help you to discern which one fits you.
- Answer the questions for each of the types and score them. The type with the highest score is the one to work with.
- If there are still several with close scores, use your life and career journey forms and your Authentic You™ Personal Learning Journal to reflect on and identify the core issue for your type. This is identified and described at the beginning of each of the chapters for the nine types.

Review information about your type and glimpse your potential

A note regarding your inner critic when working with the Enneagram, or any other assessment: The inner critic will want to focus immediately on the challenges and things that are "wrong" with this type. It will become judgmental and can shut down your learning if you focus immediately on these aspects. While they are helpful to be aware of, we intentionally focus first on your potential, in order to anchor your experience and awareness there.

Read the following short sections:

- Description of the type — first 1-2 pages of the chapter (stop at "Childhood Pattern")
- Potential for this type of person when they are most developed — read descriptions for Level 1-3 (Healthy)
- "Building on the (type's) strengths" or "The (type's) Gifts"
- "The Emergence of Essence" — last page of the chapter

---

5   Wisdom of the Enneagram, Ibid, page 13—15.

Describe your Authentic Self

Reflect on all of the responses you have gathered and the research you have completed, including your own thoughts and reflections, and compile a list of words that describe you when at your best.

Write your final list here:

Authentic Me — I am:

1.

2.

3.

4.

5.

6.

7.

8.

9.

10.

REVIEW AND REFLECT

Read the list to yourself, aloud, while looking in the mirror (or to a friend) beginning with "I am…" .

Notice how it feels and what your body language and tone are like as you do. Write down what your experience was like using the following space:

How I felt:

What I noticed about my body language and tone:

What emotions arose during this exercise, if any:

What this experience was like for me:

What I am learning about myself as a result:

Once you complete the exercises and articulate the words to describe your Authentic Self, make adjustments and transfer these into your Authentic You™ Personal Learning Journal or on to your Authentic You™ Poster. If the latter, be sure to have a second sheet so one can be for a draft copy. This will help to allay any judgments your inner critic may have about it needing to be perfect to put it on the written page.

The Egoic Mind

Thoughts, beliefs, automatic patterns

Endlessly, endlessly...
Asleep.

Once woken, "I" becomes aware of the thinker

"I am" is separate and aware
of each layer unfolding....

The observer has been observed
The suffering can now begin to lessen....

—Tana Heminsley,

— Step #2 —
Articulate your Values

Use the following action worksheet to articulate your values.

> Values are deeply held beliefs about what is important to you for your life. They are words that describe what is important to you.

"They are believed to be what people care about deeply and serve as standards for judging acts, guiding behavior, evaluating social conditions, and give meaning to life.

Values are thought to be relatively stable, much longer lasting and less subject to change than opinions so that they are not subject to sudden shifts or impulses of the moment." [6]

Finally, they can be prioritized to give emphasis to different values at different times in your life.

EXERCISES

Before beginning, center, relax and open to the exercises you are about to complete.

Review your description of Authentic Self from Step #1, reflecting on your potential and how it feels to understand who you are at your best.

Reflect on past situations and trade offs

There may have been times in your leadership career and your life when you needed to stop and consider what steps were appropriate to take next. These could have ranged from making a decision about a new career opportunity, to whether to go to university, to whether to have a family.

There are situations each day where you need to make decisions, and values — whether you know them overtly, or consider them intuitively — are providing the guideposts.

Write down two situations in which you had to take time to reflect on a decision based on your deeply held conviction about the right thing to do. For example — whether or not to take a promotion in which there would be much more time at work and travel required that would take you away from your family for the equivalent of 5 months a year.

---

6   Source: Values, http://www.orednet.org/~jflory/205/205_val_intro.htm

1.

2.

Write down words that describe what you believe in, that leads you to the criteria for making these decisions. For example—Importance of family; love of travel; love of my work; stimulation of adventure. Write your words here:

Review a list of values words

After reflecting on what values are, and some situations in your life that have required trade-offs based on what is deeply important to you, it is time to choose the words that describe your values.

COMMON PERSONAL VALUES WORDS[7]

Accomplishment, Success	Discovery	Love, Romance	Safety
Accountability	Ease of Use	Loyalty	Satisfying others
Accuracy	Efficiency	Maximum utilization	Security
Adventure	Equality	(of time, resources)	Self-givingness
All for one & one for all	Excellence	Meaning	Self-reliance
Beauty	Fairness	Merit	Service
Calm, quietude, peace	Faith	Money	(to others, society)
Challenge	Family	Openness	Simplicity
Change	Family feeling	Peace, Non-violence	Skill
Cleanliness, orderliness	Flair	Perfection (e.g. of details)	Speed
Collaboration	Freedom	Personal Growth	Spirit in life (using)
Commitment	Friendship	Pleasure	Stability
Communication	Fun	Positive attitude	Standardization
Community	Global view	Power	Status
Competence	Good will	Practicality	Strength
Competition	Goodness	Preservation	Succeed; A will to-
Concern for others	Gratitude	Privacy	Success, Achievement
Content over form	Hard work	Problem Solving	Systemization
Continuous improvement	Harmony	Progress	Teamwork
Cooperation	Honesty	Prosperity, Wealth	Timeliness
Coordination	Honor	Punctuality	Tradition
Country, love of (patriotism)	Independence	Quality of work	Tranquility
Creativity	Inner peace, calm, quietude	Regularity	Trust
Customer satisfaction	Innovation	Resourcefulness	Truth
Decisiveness	Integrity	Respect for others	Unity
Delight of being, joy	Justice	Responsiveness	Variety
Democracy	Knowledge	Results-oriented	Wisdom
Discipline	Leadership	Rule of Law	

Referring to the list, select and write down words that describe your values:

1.   5.

2.   6.

3.   7.

4.   8.

---

7   Source: Values, http://www.gurusoftware.com/GuruNet/Personal/Topics/Values.htm
For a list of Business values see: http://www.gurusoftware.com/GuruNet/Business/Values.htm

Test out your values

Think of three situations at work and in your personal life in which you need to make an important decision. Write them here. For example, *I am returning to work after maternity leave and I want to be both effective as a leader as well as with my family, and maintain my wellness;* or *I need to decide on a new product offering at work that may have potential negative impacts on a business partner I am working with.*

Situation One:

Situation Two:

Situation Three:

Next, for each of the situations, reflect on your values and what guidance they provide you. List them in order of importance to get even clearer about the emphasis you want to place on different parts of your life. Complete the following:

As I reflect on each of the above situations, my values provide the following guidance (example):

- Values (in order of importance: family, wellness, career, education, spirituality, fun)
- Situation: (Mary is returning to work after maternity leave) Mary's value of family (first priority) means that she may only want to work four days a week; her value for wellness means that she will make time for rest by booking time at the gym 3x/week for "me" time; and her value of education will have to drop in priority as she forgoes the MBA she has been thinking of doing, for the foreseeable future.

Complete your assessment using the blank table here:

My values in order of importance:	
Situation One:	
Situation Two:	
Situation Three:	

REVIEW AND REFLECT

Read the list to yourself, aloud, while looking in the mirror (or to a friend) beginning with "I value ….".

Notice how it feels and what arises for you in terms of emotions or thoughts, as you do. Write down what your experience was like using the following space:

How I felt:

What I noticed about my thoughts:

What emotions arose during this exercise, if any:

What this experience was like for me:

What I am learning about myself as a result:

Remember, this is just a starting point and your values may evolve.

They may also change in importance at different times in your life. For example, one person values travel and working hard. Then they have children they have a new value of time with family. Their focus has changed and family time "trumps" travel for the first few years of raising their children; or they may incorporate travel in a new way into their lives — instead of travelling internationally, they may choose to travel close to home, or in a way that the children can participate.

Clarity

Lightness
Spaciousness
Balance

Calm, serene, cool...

Physically lighter,
the body regains balance

The mind opens to the
brilliance of life.

Colors are at their fullest intensity
energy vibrates and is available...

All becomes clear....

—Tana Heminsley,

— Step #3 —
Discover your Purpose

Use the following action worksheet to articulate your purpose.

Authentic leaders are clear about what their higher purpose is, or what they were intended for in their life.

> Your purpose is the reason beyond yourself that provides meaning for your life. It is how you are meant to leave your mark in the world—how you are meant to contribute, and your legacy for your family.

In order to become clear about your purpose, there are several things you can do.

EXERCISES

Begin by relaxing, centering and opening to the exercises you are about to complete.

Review your research from Steps #1 and #2

Review your material from Step #1: Articulating Authentic Self: the life review, the information from friends, family, and co-workers, as well as the results of your personality assessments. In addition, review your values. Reflect on how it feels to understand who you are at your best and what is important to you.

Then, complete the following statements:

My strengths are (what I'm good at and what I love)…

When I do the following activities, I notice that my energy builds…

I love contributing by doing the following…

My passion in life is…

My higher purpose is…

If you are unclear, review and complete the following:

Conduct interviews

Conduct informal interviews with at least three people who are living their lives and contributing in ways that you are curious about or interested in. (For example, you know a person who has started a business in ecotourism and you have always been curious about it—especially as the person was formerly a doctor and in her/his late 40s is when the life change took place; another person is a lawyer and you think you might like to be a lawyer and represent people when they have been in an accident; another person has written a book about time management and effective organizing; another makes jewellery for a living.)

Ask them to have or tea/coffee with you or set up a call or face-to-face meeting. Ask if they will be willing to share their story and insights with you. For each person, ask them the following questions and record your responses here:

Question:	Person One:
Can you describe what it is that you do?	
How is what you do meaningful to you?	
How did you get to where you are? What has been your journey?	
What made you make the changes to your life?	
What things would I need to consider if I were to do something similar? What are the challenges with what you do?	

Question:	Person One:
What do you love about living this way?	
What does a typical day in your life look like?	
What does the typical month look like?	

Question:	Person Two:
Can you describe what it is that you do?	
How is what you do meaningful to you?	
How did you get to where you are? What has been your journey?	
What made you make the changes to your life?	
What things would I need to consider if I were to do something similar?	
What are the challenges with what you do?	
What do you love about living this way?	
What does a typical day in your life look like?	
What does the typical month look like?	

Question:	Person Three:
Can you describe what it is that you do?	
How is what you do meaningful to you?	
How did you get to where you are? What has been your journey?	
What made you make the changes to your life?	
What things would I need to consider if I were to do something similar?	
What are the challenges with what you do?	
What do you love about living this way?	
What does a typical day in your life look like?	
What does the typical month look like?	

After you have conducted the interviews, ask yourself the following questions, and record your responses here:

What I notice:	Person One:
Does thinking about this as a possibility excite me for my life?	
Is there other information I need to gather about their occupation?	
Does my energy build or diminish when I hear about the way this person is living?	

What I notice:	Person Two:
Does thinking about this as a possibility excite me for my life?	
Is there other information I need to gather about their occupation?	
Does my energy build or diminish when I hear about the way this person is living?	

What I notice:	Person Three:
Does thinking about this as a possibility excite me for my life?	
Is there other information I need to gather about their occupation?	
Does my energy build or diminish when I hear about the way this person is living?	

Shift or let go of self-limiting beliefs

You may have a difficult time seeing new possibilities for your leadership and your life if you can only imagine one way forward—the way it has always been, or if you notice that you have lots of reasons why something different is just not possible.

Review the chapter on inner development, as well as the action worksheet for creating your Inner Development Plan. You may need to spend several months working on shifting beliefs before you see different possibilities for what you are intended for or what your purpose is.

If you are not sure how to proceed, your Inner Development Plan may include one thing—find a trusted person to get support from for a targeted period of time.

Create your Purpose

Remind your inner critic that this is just a draft, and so you can let go of the pressure it will want to put on you. Combine what you have written above into a list and write it here.

My purpose in the world is to do the following:

Point one:

Point two:

Point three:

Next, combine these points into one statement — My purpose in the world is to do the following:

REVIEW AND REFLECT

Read the statement to yourself aloud, while looking in the mirror (or to a friend) beginning with "My purpose is ….".

Notice how it feels and what arises for you in terms of emotions or thoughts, as you do. Write down what your experience was like using the following space:

How I felt:

What I noticed about my thoughts:

What emotions arose during this exercise, if any:

What this experience was like for me:

What I am learning about myself as a result:

Leave the statement for a few days and adjust it until it feels aligned with who you are. When it represents who you are, you will experience a sense of calm and deep knowing — a feeling of coming home.

Emotions - Learning to Feel

Starting out as unseen, unfelt
Knowing something is out of alignment
And yet, not having the language to
describe it

Beginners mind
learning the language
while building capacity to stay present
with the discomfort of
each feeling...
each emotion....

The wave builds and
then lets go
the emotion is experienced
as a building and
receding...
expansion and
contraction...
positive and
negative...
experienced without preference.

This too shall pass...

—Tana Heminsley

— Step #4 —
Clarify your Leadership Principles

Use the following action worksheet to articulate your leadership principles.

> Leadership principles are specific, tactical statements that help to articulate how to translate Authentic Self, values, and your higher purpose into your day-to-day activities.

Leadership principles have been described as "values translated into action".[8]

Authentic leaders use leadership principles to live in alignment with their Authentic Self, their values, and their purpose on a day-to-day basis.

Leadership principles are broad enough to cross industries and businesses, and specific enough to provide guidance for your day-to-day activities. They support you to tactically translate your personal clarity and intrinsic motivators, to being able to lead and live authentically.

Your Authentic Self description, values, purpose and leadership principles may hold relatively constant in your life. What may change over time are the specific jobs you choose in your career.

When you are clear about what is important to you, your criteria for choosing positions become clear as well. When in jobs that are congruent with your Authentic Self, you are more engaged and effective at what you do.

There are several things you can do to clarify your leadership principles.

EXERCISES

Begin by relaxing, centering and opening to the exercises you are about to complete.

Complete a self-reflection

Reflect on your what you've learned about your Authentic Self, values and your higher purpose.

Answer the following questions and write your responses below:

---

8   Bill George, True North, p 86.

When I am being my Authentic Self, without the limiting voices of my personality, the "shoulds", or my inner critic, what is it that I love to do at work or in my business?

What do I love to do that will support creating a great environment where people I work with can feel comfortable to be authentic as well?

How will I contribute to making the world a better place through my business practices?

How will these business practices contribute to abundance for the business, the world, and myself?

Create a list of leadership principles

Once you have reflected on these questions, create a list of words or statements that are your leadership principles — how your Authentic Self, your Values and your Higher Purpose for your life translates into your day-to-day activities.

These principles are transferable across industries or organizations, as well as in your personal life, and they provide a way to bring forth your Authentic Self, more of the time.

The following are examples of leadership principles for two different people:

Person One:

Authentic Self/ Purpose:	
Authentic Self: Creative, Entrepreneurial, Self-aware, Inspiring, Courageous Purpose: Supporting people to be the best they can be	
Value:	**Leadership Principle:**
Authenticity	Talk about the importance of authenticity when having conversations and model it in your leadership—both 1:1 and in groups; with peers, direct reports and supervisors; and with customers.
Sustainability	Creating the conditions for a low-to-no carbon footprint; modeling it in your own behaviours for your team and in your personal life.
Connection	Facilitating team-building workshops where people can develop community as they learn about their potential as a person.

Person Two:

Authentic Self/ Purpose:	
Authentic Self: Direct, Loyal, Gets things done, Intensely committed, Witty, Inventor Purpose: To leave a legacy for my children.	
Value:	**Leadership Principle:**
Financial security	Ensure the return on investment is clearly articulated and understood before the investment is agreed to, and, Support team members to understand financial concepts and how they support decision making.
Education	Creating the conditions for life-long learning.
Family	Encourage "family first" philosophy with my employees and clients.

Your Authentic Self description, values, purpose and leadership principles may hold relatively constant in your life. What may change over time are the specific jobs you choose in your career.

Another leader who has "connection" as a value, and a purpose of "supporting people to be the best they can be", might have a leadership principle of "Facilitating team-building workshops where people can develop community as they learn about their potential as a person".

There is a transferable principle that this leader can take to any job or volunteer position at any time.

When you are clear about what is important to you, your criteria for choosing positions become clear as well. When in jobs that are congruent with your Authentic Self, your are more engaged and effective at what you do.

My leadership principles are:

Authentic Self/Purpose:	
Value:	**Leadership Principle:**

Use your leadership principles each day

Using the list of leadership principles you created; plan to incorporate them into your day-to-day activities by completing the following:

List the current activities I do in my job:

Review the list and reflect on the following:

What percentage of the activities I do each day are aligned with my principles?

What can I do differently to bring a higher percentage of my day-to-day leadership activities into alignment with my leadership principles?

Are there activities that do not align, that I can given away to someone else who likes to do them? Who else could do the activities for me?

Is there any support I would need to have in order to implement my leadership principles?

Suggestions for incorporating your principles into your day-to-day leadership include:

- Review them with 1 or 2 trusted friends, family or peers and ask for feedback. Add anything you may have missed.
- Communicate these to your peers, boss and team.
- Integrate these principles and what you are learning about yourself into your organizational leadership development processes (talent management, performance management) annually.
- Use your Authentic Self description, values, purpose and principles to guide your career advancement.
- Practice leading using your principles.
- Adjust them as you evolve and grow.

REVIEW AND REFLECT

Read the statement to yourself aloud, while looking in the mirror (or to a friend) beginning with "My leadership principles are …".

Notice how it feels and what arises for you in terms of emotions or thoughts, as you do. Write down what your experience was like using the following space:

How I felt:

What I noticed about my thoughts:

What emotions arose during this exercise, if any:

What this experience was like for me:

What I am learning about myself as a result:

Spaciousness

Clarity

Lightness

A broad sense of the expansiveness
before me.

The universe.

Each time I wake up
the resistance lets go...

I settle and
breathe

A sigh of relief...

And open to the
spaciousness of life.

—Tana Heminsley

— Step #5—
Create your Life Vision

Use the following action worksheet to articulate your vision for your life.

> Your life vision is the articulation of what your optimal life looks like. It includes all parts of your life including personal and work.

It can be created visually as a collage and/or by writing down the themes that emerge. You can complete it using a poster board and magazines or you can use online tools that are available if you Google them. You could also write a poem or create a song.

Use whatever creative modality that will support you to express your optimal life! This is the first step to creating the life you want to live.

A Life Vision Board is one tool that you can use to create yours. It involves a collage of images, colours and words that help to remind you and anchor you to the qualities of, and activities in, the life you want to create.

After it is created, you need only to spend time reflecting on it. This will guide you to choose and take steps that move your day-to-day experience further in alignment with your vision.

EXERCISES

Begin by relaxing, centering and opening to the exercises you are about to complete.

Reflect on what you have learned

Reflect on your what you've learned about your Authentic Self, values and purpose and leadership principles.

Gather your materials and Create your Life Vision Board

Complete the following steps to create your life vision board:

a) Gather 5-6 magazines that represent who you are at this point in your life, family photos that are meaningful, and other materials that you might want to incorporate into a collage. Purchase a poster board (in a colour that speaks to you) and gather together a pair of scissors, some scotch tape, and some coloured pens.

Put on your most comfortable clothing, find a space that feels energizing for you to create in, and put on your favourite music. Give yourself up to 2 hours (or whatever is needed) to create your life-vision board.

Note: While this is a lovely exercise to do with your partner or significant other, it can be helpful to leave that for later. For now, the focus is creating your vision.

b) (optional) Complete the following short visualization exercise.

Close your eyes and either sit in a comfortable chair, or lie down on the floor on a yoga mat, or on a sofa. Spend 10-30 minutes thinking of a perfect day in your life in the future. Ask yourself the following:

- What does it look like?
- What do you experience?
- What does it feel like?
- What are all the activities that are occurring at this moment in your life vision?
- How does it include your personal life? Your Work-life?

After your visualization exercise, bring your awareness back into the room and begin your creation.

c) Flip through the magazines and other materials you have gathered, paying attention to images and words that call to you. This is a right-brain exercise so remind yourself to let go of analyzing for the moment as you enjoy creating. Cut the images and words out and set aside.

d) Once you have gathered all the images and words that feel right at this time, begin to assemble them on the poster board and tape them in place as a collage. After you have completed your life-vision board, write your name and the date in one corner or the board so you remember when you created it.

In the future, as you make more life-vision boards, you will be able to follow how they change over time.

REVIEW AND REFLECT

Review the story of your life-vision board aloud to yourself (or to a friend or significant other) beginning with "My life vision is ....".

Notice how it feels and what arises for you in terms of emotions or thoughts, as you do. Write down what your experience was like using the following space:

How I felt:

What I noticed about my thoughts:

What emotions arose during this exercise, if any:

What this experience was like for me:

What I am learning about myself as a result:

Notice how it feels to practice being vulnerable and sharing something deeply important to you with another person.

Review your life vision board on a regular basis (some spend time with it each day) and then put it away. By reminding yourself about it and leaving it on the back burner so it can "percolate" and bubble away, you are allowing the next steps on your path to emerge.

Once you have achieved a major milestone in your life (this may be years later), review the life vision board again and see how your actions relate to the vision you created.

It is common for people to share with others that they are amazed that something that they put on their life vision board, and then completely forgot about, has come to fruition in their life.

Exhaustion

Keep going
So much to do
Have to get it done...

For what?....Really?

When there are sunsets to savor
And favorite people to be with...

A sigh of relief as the spaciousness
of the universe breathes my body.....

Letting go of ego
No longer victim.

I step into "being"...

And sleep.

— Tana Heminsley,

— Step #6—
Assess your Work-Life Balance

Use the following action worksheet to assess your current vs. optimal work-life balance.

> Work-life balance occurs when you have an understanding of the different parts of your life and the relative emphasis and time you would like to dedicate to each. This will be different over time as priorities and life changes.

Authentic leaders have a sense of calm about them. They are able to maintain perspective and balance all parts of their lives, more of the time. They have wellness practices that are foundational to their ability to maintain perspective, particularly in uncomfortable or new situations. Authentic leaders live and lead thoughtfully and make time for reflection and "white space" in their week. Their priorities for work-life balance change as they move through new chapters in their lives. Their sense of balance is flexible, knowing that in order to be in balance, they may first be out of balance—a reminder that progress is not just linear.

Mastering work-life balance can support authenticity. First take stock of your current life balance—how you think about it, and how you are balancing your time.

EXERCISES

Begin by relaxing, centering and opening to the exercises you are about to complete.

Reflect on what you have learned

Reflect on what you've learned about your Authentic Self, values, purpose, leadership principles and life vision. This provides the context for understanding the awakening that may be occurring, as well as assessing your current vs. optimal work-life balance.

Complete your Work-life Balance Assessment

Refer to the following diagram and complete the exercise below.

Work-life balance assessment—example of one person's current level of work-life balance:

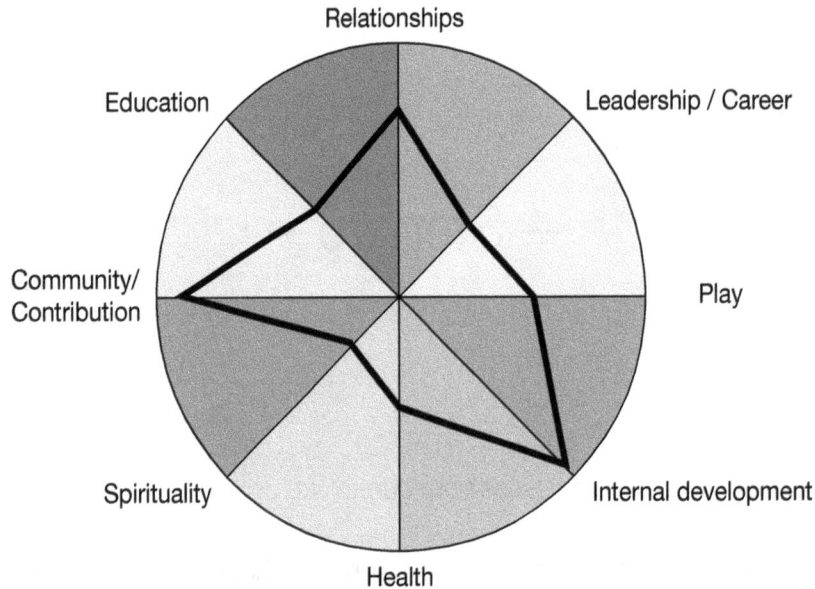

This diagram shows, in a simple way, the different areas of this person's life and the amount of effort/energy they are spending in each of them. The outside of the circle is the optimal level and the point on each line for each piece of the "pie" of your life shows the current level for each area.

The diagram gives an indication about how this leader may be feeling out of balance and where may want to make adjustments. For example, this person is happy with the level of energy/time spent on community and contribution, relationships, and internal development. One area to focus on for improvement is health and spirituality.

Instructions for completing your work-life balance assessment

a) Step one, identify and name the different parts of your life — relationships, career, contribution, abundance — use your own words/labels for what is meaningful for you.

b) Step two, assume the outer edge of the circle is your optimal amount of that component in your life (i.e. you want to have some education in your life through continuing education at your community college, but you don't want to pursue a PhD). Assume the centre of the circle is a 0 and the outer edge is a 10. This provides a simple way of showing the relative importance of each component to you.

c) Step three, draw a line from the centre of the circle to the outer edge, for each part of your life. Place a dot on the line for each component to show where you are currently. For example in the diagram above, it shows community/contribution as about an 8 out of 10. This means that the person currently has quite a lot of this relative to, say, health. When they assess their whole life, they may want to make adjustments to focus more on health. Or maybe not. The system is designed to be flexible and to fit each person's life and language — there are no judgments attached (that one is better than another) — this is merely the current state.

d) Step four, once you have a dot on each line, join them with a line to show the relative "balance" in your life currently.

e) Step five, reflect on what this tells you as you become more self-aware. Think about what lifestyle adjustments you might want to make, if any, to shift the balance to one that is optimal for you at this time.

My current life balance:

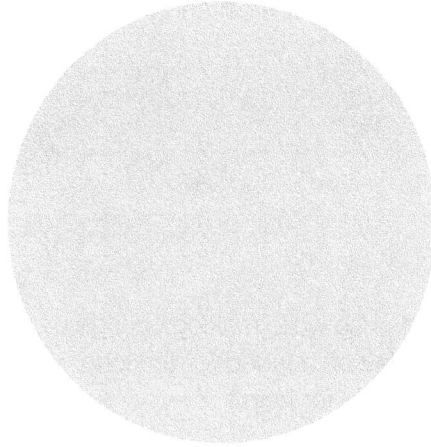

Choose what to improve

Decide on two or three parts of your life you'd like to adjust in order to have more balance. Write your response here.

Given my values and my current balance, some areas of my life where I would like to adjust my balance would be _____, _____, and _____. (i.e. career, health and play)

Decide on the level of improvement

Consider the following questions and write down your responses, as you reflect on what will be needed in order to make adjustments.

What are the realities (family and business) and needs to consider and respect when looking at possibilities for trade-offs?

Do I know all the possible solutions? If not, who could support me to think through them? (i.e. we have a large project coming up for which I'll have to work weekends for the next 2 months — I'll need to check with my peers/boss in case this may go longer).

What will be the trade-offs if I make adjustments and how can my values help me decide the right way to make the adjustment? (i.e. for the next 2 months I may need to ask my parents to support my partner and me by taking our child for 1 day a weekend; I'll book a long weekend away with my family once the project is over).

What challenges or obstacles might arise while making changes to have more balance? (i.e. I may not be used to asking my boss for the day off needed for the long weekend I want to book; I may not be used to asking my parents—or friends — for help.)

Decide Who will support you

What support might I need? Whom could I ask to support me?

Create a simple plan

My simple plan for beginning to practice balance in my life (keep it simple so it's more realistic):

The Belief about balance I will need to shift, plus the Benefit:
Belief I'll need to shift: More time for me to rest (as work consists of back-to-back meetings and we have 2 kids) Benefit: I'll be more effective as a boss and a parent as I'll have more perspective and feel less resentful.
How I will reframe this belief:
That time to care for myself is important. Also, that I value myself enough to book the time and follow through in order to keep the promise to myself.
Action I will take:
Book 1.5 hours a week to go for a walk in the forest on my own (or go for coffee, or to the spa, etc.)
Support I will need:
Someone to take the kids so I can keep my commitment to myself.
Conversations I will need to have:
• Set a boundary for meetings — instead of 60 minutes with no breaks in between, make them 45 minutes with a 10 minute break. • Ask my partner to support me when I want to let go of this promise to myself. • Ask my partner how I can support her in booking time for herself as well.

Create your plan here. There are spaces for plans for up to 5 values on the next pages.

The Belief about balance I will need to shift, plus the Benefit:
How I will reframe this belief:
Action I will take:
Support I will need:
Conversations I will need to have:

The Belief about balance I will need to shift, plus the Benefit:

How I will reframe this belief:

Action I will take:

Support I will need:

Conversations I will need to have:

The Belief about balance I will need to shift, plus the Benefit:

How I will reframe this belief:

Action I will take:

Support I will need:

Conversations I will need to have:

The Belief about balance I will need to shift, plus the Benefit:
How I will reframe this belief:
Action I will take:
Support I will need:
Conversations I will need to have:

The Belief about balance I will need to shift, plus the Benefit:

How I will reframe this belief:

Action I will take:

Support I will need:

Conversations I will need to have:

REVIEW AND REFLECT

Review your Work-Life Balance Assessment and reflect on what it tells you.

Notice how it feels and what arises for you in terms of emotions or thoughts. Write down what your experience was like using the following space:

How I felt:

What I noticed about my thoughts:

What emotions arose during this exercise, if any:

What this experience was like for me:

What I am learning about myself as a result:

Constant surrendering

Easing into surrendering

Easing into life

Like sliding into the warmth of the water
in the bathtub

Settling in and feeling the warmth
envelope me...

Feeling held
Feeling supported

Experiencing life
as it unfolds with ease....

—Tana Heminsley,

— Step #7 —
Reflect on the Awakening
and Implications for your Leadership

Use the following action worksheet to understand the awakening that may be created when you completed the first six steps of the Authentic You™ Personal Planning System and renewed your personal clarity. Also reflect on the implications for your leadership.

> An awakening occurs when you learn something new about yourself that is startlingly different than what you believe to be true.

EXERCISES

Reflect on what you have learned

Reflect on your what you've learned about your Authentic Self, values, purpose, leadership principles, life vision and work-life balance assessment. Next, complete the following questions:

What are you learning about your life and how you would like to live aligned with Authentic Self? What are you becoming awake to?

How important is what you are learning about yourself? How is it important to you?

What are you learning about your leadership and how you would like to bring your Authentic Self into your day-to-day activities?

What are the implications for your leadership? What will you focus on for the next 3 months? For the next 12 months?

What are two strengths that will support you as you move forward?

What are two self-limiting beliefs that will be helpful to shift or let go of, in order for you to move forward? How can you reframe them to improve your leadership?

Is there any support you would need to have in order to be more authentic in your leadership?

REVIEW AND REFLECT

Read your responses to yourself. Notice how it feels and what arises for you in terms of emotions or thoughts. Write a statement that describes your awakening, and your understanding of the implications for your leadership and your life.

The awakening is:

The implications for my leadership are:

The implications for my life are:

Write down what your experience was like using the following space:

How I felt:

What I noticed about my thoughts:

What emotions arose during this exercise, if any:

What this experience was like for me:

What I am learning about myself as a result:

Trust

I have it all
Right now
Inside of me...

No need to fret
To over prepare
Or let anxiousness overtake....

Ease in and trust
Be with what is
"I" lives through me
In the present, every moment.

Let go of struggle!
Live in celebration.
Live with ease....

Trust.

—Tana Heminsley,

— Step #8 —
Set your Goals

Use the following action worksheet to develop your goals (personal and business).

> A Goal is a specific and measureable description of something you want to achieve or change. Alternatively an Intention is where you set your mind to achieving or changing something, though you do not get specific in how you describe it (i.e. it doesn't include a measure or target, just a general statement of your intention).

EXERCISES

Reflect on what you have learned

Reflect on your what you've learned about your Authentic Self, values, purpose, leadership principles and life vision (including any business or other goals you would like to set) and complete the following exercise:

a) Choose a time horizon that feels right for your life (i.e. 6 months, one year).

The time horizon that feels right for me is: _____

b) Review the work-life balance assessment you completed and decide on the two to three areas in which you would like to see something different (i.e. the three lowest ratings for where you are currently spending your energy compared to the optimal level. For the example above it is career, spirituality and health).

The parts of my life I would like to see change are:

1.

2.

3.

Setting goals or intentions

Set a goal or an intention for each of these parts of your life that will provide focus for your choices and actions for the next applicable timeframe. Make the goal as specific and clear as possible. Intentions are more general and set the tone and provide a theme for the next timeframe.

Examples of goals include:

- Career/Business—Increase gross sales to $5M annually by December.
- Personal Development—Find a community of support by September and attend 6 group sessions by December.
- Health—practice yoga 2-3 times per week for an hour—have a consistent practice by May.

Examples of intentions are:

- Career/business—to improve sales by cultivating exceptional customer experiences
- Personal development—find a community and practice accepting support
- Health—to create the conditions for a renewed sense of strength and wellness

1. Area of my life I would like to see change occur in:
   Goal or intention:

2. Area of my life I would like to see change occur in:
   Goal or intention:

3. Area of my life I would like to see change occur in:
   Goal or intention:

Record these in your Authentic Leadership Authentic You™ Personal Learning Journal™ or on the poster (so you have all your information on one page).

Taking action

Decide on one action that is the next step that you can take to achieve your goals—this can be for the next day, week, month, quarter, or however long you think you need to complete this step. Record these as well. Some examples are:

- Career/Business: Implement the social networking strategy in the next month (by June).
- Spirituality: Talk to 3 people whom I admire, and ask them how they include spirituality in their life (if they do) and where they find their community of support (by July).
- Health: Sign up for a monthly package at a yoga studio or download a free Yoga App on my SmartPhone (by April 15).

1. Goal or intention:
   One action I will take to move forward:

2. Goal or intention:
   One action I will take to move forward:

3. Goal or intention:
   One action I will take to move forward:

REVIEW AND REFLECT

Review your goals and reflect on the implications for your life. Are they realistic? Achievable? At a level of difficulty that is within 10% of your comfort zone?

Notice how it feels and what arises for you in terms of emotions or thoughts. Write down what your experience was like using the following space:

How I felt:

What I noticed about my thoughts:

What emotions arose during this exercise, if any:

What this experience was like for me:

What I am learning about myself as a result:

Review your goals on a regular basis and reflect on whether they need to be adjusted or whether you have achieved them. Make adjustments where necessary.

Dates I will review my goals and/or intentions in order to keep them fresh and clear:

Date:

Date:

Date:

Date:

Anger

Fiery hot anger!
Never before seen...
Let alone felt....

Pushed down and down
into the dark abyss of
the shadow
the unseen
the unfelt
the unacknowledged.

And then...one day...
Miraculously...I take a look....

A quick glimpse...and I feel
where it lives in my body.

I stay with it
I am curious about it
it is as if I'm comforting it...

And the shift occurs
it is gone...
until the next time....

—Tana Heminsley,

— Step #9—

Create your Inner Development Plan

Use the following action worksheet to create your Inner Development Plan.

> Your inner development plan focuses on awareness and self-managing to have more choice about the thoughts, emotions and physiological sensations you pay attention to, the guidance they provide, and the choices for your behaviours as you align them with your Authentic Self.

Creating a development plan for the inner development begins with an understanding of what goals you want to accomplish and an awareness of limiting beliefs and behaviours that might be getting in the way.

You may be able to complete all or part of your Inner Development Plan on your own, and/or it may be helpful to work with a guide who can see potential blind spots. This could include your supervisor, a friend, a mentor, and/or a coach.

EXERCISES

Begin by relaxing, centering and opening to the exercises you are about to complete.

Reflect on what you have learned

Reflect on your what you've learned about your Authentic Self, values, purpose, leadership principles, life vision, work-life balance, goals, and answer the following question:

Given who I am at my best and what I want to accomplish, both at work and at home, are there any beliefs or behaviours that if I shifted them or let them go, would support me at this time?

Review the following example and, using your goals, identify limiting beliefs and/or behaviours below:

My goal:	Limiting belief or behaviour:
Learn how to delegate more effectively within 3 months.	Impatience with others who complete tasks differently than you would; judging other approaches — believing that using a different approach than yours will not produce as good a result.

Next, research what exercises you can do to achieve each goal and to create new behaviours that will support achieving it. In addition, identify exercises you can complete for awareness and self-management.

Use the following table of examples for ideas, and Inner Development Plan form to complete your plan.

Inner Development Plan — Ideas for exercises

The following table shows several pages of sample goals within an organizational context (for situations that are frequently learning "edges" for leaders at one time or another in their career), as well as sample actions and exercises for your Inner Development Plan.

Consider these exercises for your Authentic You™ Personal Planning System if you are having challenges in these areas. Note — for most examples in this table the timeframe is 3 months. This may vary depending on the amount of time required to actually achieve the internal shifts required and to create the new behaviours. As you begin to understand the length of time needed for yourself, you can adjust the time in your Inner Development Plan.

Your goal:
Learn how to delegate more effectively — within 3 months.
Limiting belief or behaviour and mindset shift required:
Impatience with others who complete tasks differently than you would have; judging other approaches — believing that using a different approach than yours will not produce as good a result. Mindset shift required — To see delegation as essential to your effectiveness, and getting things done through others as efficient rather than an extra effort. Delegating also gives the other person the chance to shine!
Exercises to help shift or let go of it:
Each week create a list of 5 things that need to get done, who can complete them (not you), and what support you can provide so they learn. Assign the task and support the person as they complete it.
Exercises for awareness and self-managing:
Awareness — Pay attention to what happens for you (i.e. your anxiousness, lack of trust, and desire to take the work back and do it yourself) when the person completes the work differently from how you would have. Self-managing — Practice self-managing and talk to the person with a non-judgmental tone in order to check understanding; provide feedback and ask them to make the changes themselves.

Your goal:
Improve your ability to give up resources when this is the right answer for the company — within 1 week.
Limiting belief or behaviour and mindset shift required:
Blaming peers in other departments for getting resources that you wanted to acquire for your own projects. Mindset shift required — Doing the right thing for the customer and company is essential. Use the company vision and values as a starting point for working together; collaboration between departments is the key.
Exercises to help shift or let go of it:
In your resource allocation meeting, practice giving up one thing that is low risk for your team.
Exercises for awareness and self-managing:
Awareness — Pay attention to the process — what occurs in your mind. The process of blaming may arise in this discussion. The content may be blaming because you believe the person doesn't value you and you judge yourself as weak if you give up any resources. Self-managing — Notice what happens for you internally when you give up the resource, and what the reaction is of the person you give it to. Reflect on the benefits for the team and the company. Debrief this experience with your supervisor and do one thing personally to celebrate your willingness to shift.

Your goal:
Be a more effective manager — within 3 months.
Limiting belief or behaviour and mindset shift required:
Getting defensive when people disagree with you or challenge your assumptions. Mindset shift required — Realizing you are doing something right to create a great environment in which people feel safe enough to share their opinions, particularly when they may cause disagreement. Thank them for challenging you.
Exercises to help shift or let go of it:
In 1:1 and group interactions, encourage team members to disagree with you and to challenge your assumptions in order to ensure that you have more complete information for decision making.
Exercises for awareness and self-managing:
Awareness — Pay attention to what happens in your body (thoughts, emotions) when others challenge you. Using The Wisdom of the Enneagram book, review the Levels of Development for your personality type, to understand what your healthy levels look like, and review the exercises suggested for when your type is under stress. Reflect on what your automatic pattern is. Self-managing — Practice deepening your breathing and staying open to hearing what other people have to say. Watch your tone and body language as you respond. Practice letting go of judgments as they arise and ask questions to clarify your understanding.

Your goal:
Improve your communication skills in difficult or uncomfortable situations — within 3 months.
Limiting belief or behaviour and mindset shift required:
Avoiding difficult conversations and/or being unaware of their impact on others. Mindset shift required — Difficult conversations are opportunities to strengthen a relationship; they get less difficult with practice.
Exercises to help shift or let go of it:
Practice clearing issues within 24 hours of when they occur, so they don't become big issues.
Exercises for awareness and self-managing:
Awareness — Pay attention to your current pattern and how you think about clearing issues. (Do you avoid them at all cost? Do you get angry and defensive and show it in your tone and body language?) Self-managing — Practice using the arc of intense energy model to breathe and stay present through the conversation while you clear the issue.

Your goal:
Improve your healthy debating skills in Leadership Team meetings on highly contentious strategic issues — within 3 months.
Limiting belief or behaviour and mindset shift required:
A fear of debating; seeing it as aggressive Mindset shift required — As an introvert, you can learn to enjoy debating as a kind of healthy sparring to come up with the best solution — just keep it focused on ideas rather than people.
Exercises to help shift or let go of it:
In each team meeting, prepare prior to the meeting and write down ideas for questions. Ask three questions and then state your opinion.
Exercises for awareness and self-managing:
Awareness - Notice what occurs for you in your body when you interact with team members. Notice your assumptions about their reactions and practice staying present through uncomfortable feelings that may arise. Self-managing - Practice deep breathing and relaxing as you continue to engage in the conversation. After the meeting reflect on one thing you did well and one thing you could have done differently. Incorporate these learnings in the next team meeting.

Your goal:
Practice focus and discipline for more effective time management — within 3 months.
Limiting belief or behaviour and mindset shift required:
Avoiding planning; not thinking strategically. Mindset shift required—Ongoing time to step back to see the forest, will allow you to be more effective when you go back into the day-to-day of walking amongst the trees.
Exercises to help shift or let go of it:
Using your Authentic You™ Personal Planning System (particularly your purpose and life vision) as context, once each quarter, practice prioritizing and planning for the next month, quarter and the balance of the year.
Exercises for awareness and self-managing:
Awareness - Pay attention to how you think about planning and whether you value it or not. If you do not value it, practice thinking about it in a different way—in a way that allows you to be enthusiastic about, it or at the least accept that planning will support you to be more effective. Before doing the planning exercise, reflect on how you can do it, and where, so that it aligns with your purpose and life vision (i.e. you can do it on a weekend away, or you can make your favorite meal as a celebration once it is complete). Reflect on how you currently plan, and how it would feel if it you did it in a way that is aligned with your authentic self. Self-managing – When you are planning and you notice discomfort, practice self-managing to be aware of what is coming up for you. Reflect on what is behind the discomfort and what you are learning about yourself as a result.

My Inner Development Plan:

Your goal:
Limiting belief or behaviour and mindset shift required:
Exercises to help shift or let go of it:
Exercises for awareness and self-managing:

Your goal:
Limiting belief or behaviour and mindset shift required:
Exercises to help shift or let go of it:
Exercises for awareness and self-managing:

Your goal:
Limiting belief or behaviour and mindset shift required:
Exercises to help shift or let go of it:
Exercises for awareness and self-managing:

Your goal:

Limiting belief or behaviour and mindset shift required:

Exercises to help shift or let go of it:

Exercises for awareness and self-managing:

Your goal:
Limiting belief or behaviour and mindset shift required:
Exercises to help shift or let go of it:
Exercises for awareness and self-managing:

REVIEW AND REFLECT

Review your Inner Development Plan. Notice how it feels and what arises for you in terms of emotions or thoughts. Write down what your experience was like using the following space:

How I felt:

What I noticed about my thoughts:

What emotions arose during this exercise, if any:

What this experience was like for me:

What I am learning about myself as a result:

Authentic Leadership Conversations™

Relationships emerge and deepen
Alchemy takes hold

Spaciousness in the dialogue
Awakening continues

A breath of fresh air
Supportive and encouraging

A new way of being

Leadership Capacity strengthens
Participants leave

Full of hope
and newly grounded....

—Tana Heminsley,

Putting it into Practice

Use the following action worksheet to put your Authentic You™ Personal Planning System into practice.

> Putting it into Practice includes deciding when you will review the materials, how often, and who will support you along the way.

Now that you have your first iteration of the Authentic You™ Personal Planning System completed, what do you do with it?

This system is helpful both the first time you use it for gaining personal clarity, as well as on an ongoing basis for the rest of your life. It is meant to provide the foundation for your inner guidance system to help you constantly recalibrate your orientation to living as your Authentic Self. This is especially helpful in a world of ambiguity and change where staying true to yourself is the essential, and sometimes more difficult, path.

After completing the system for the first time, you can review and revise your answers whenever you like. The timing for these reviews may be different for you than for others. You get to choose the pace. You may find it helpful to revisit your Authentic You™ Personal Planning System on a regular basis (monthly or annually), and/or whenever the need arises. For some, an annual review is helpful, for others they simply wait until the next time that feels right arises.

If you have the opportunity to integrate the system, into your career planning and performance management conversations, an annual review fits with these organizational processes. To honor your authenticity, though, it is recommended that you choose a review option that is aligned with your values and goals, and pay attention to how the timing feels. This may or may not coincide with your organization's schedule. If it feels out of alignment with your Authentic Self—too rushed or not frequent enough—simply choose a different pace. Remember, you have creative control of your life!

EXERCISES

a) Decide on how often you will do a complete review of your Authentic You™ Personal Planning System and Authentic You™ Personal Learning Journal. Will it be monthly, quarterly, annually?

Complete your review by re-doing each step. Make any changes to improve your Work-life balance, or set a different goal, as you become aware of a next self-limiting belief or behaviour, that would be helpful to shift.

b) Once you have completed the review, make adjustments in your Personal Learning Journal or create a new Authentic You™ Poster.

Reflect on how these changes feel. Notice what you are learning about yourself as you undertake this exercise and share your learnings with someone you trust and can be yourself with.

c) Another time to do a wholesale review is when you are at a crossroads in your life or career, or when a major life event has occurred. In addition, there may be a time when it simply feels right.

Review all the components of your Authentic You™ Personal Planning System and make adjustments where required. Notice how different possibilities for the future show up and how your choices and actions take on a new focus as a result.

d) Share the changes with others you feel comfortable with — family and friends, and members of your community of support.

Community of Support

Complete the following to create your community of support.

Reflect on who you have in your life who would be willing to support you on your journey to living as your Authentic Self. You may or may not have a community of support already in place. Write their names here:

Research communities of support that feel aligned to your values and life vision, and leadership principles. If you cannot find one, you may want to create one. List five people who might be interested in participating as a peer-mentoring group or community of support:

1.

2.

3.

4.

5.

List your Personal Board of Directors or Dream Team members as well as the kind of advice and guidance you seek them out for:

Who:	What guidance you see them out for:	When you will meet with them next:

Choose people with whom there is an alignment of values, with whom your energy builds when you are around them, who inspire you to be a better person and with whom you want to be in relationship for many years.

Notice how it is to be choiceful about whom you spend time with.

Reflect on what you are learning about yourself and write down your thoughts here:

Personal Learning Journal

Use the following pages to summarize what you discovered as you completed each step of the Authentic You™ Personal Planning System. Once you have completed each Action Worksheet, transfer the final product into the Personal Learning Journal, and/or onto your Authentic You™ Poster.

1. My Authentic Self
2. My Values
3. My Purpose
4. My Leadership Principles
5. My Life Vision
6. My Work-Life Balance
7. My Awakening
8. My Goals
9. My Inner Development Plan
10. My Community of Support

Authentic You™ Personal Planning System
Personal Learning Journal

Date:_____

My Authentic Self

Knowing who I am when being my authentic self provides a glimpse of who I am when at my best – my potential....

When I am my best or authentic self I am:

My Values

My values define my core and most deeply held beliefs. They provide guidance for my thoughts, behaviours and decision making....

I value:

My Purpose

My purpose clarifies what I am intended for in my life. It gives me meaning and defines the gifts I bring to others. It helps focus my choices....

My purpose is:

My Leadership Principles

My leadership principles translate my personal clarity about authentic self, values and purpose, into how I want each day to look....

My leadership principles:

My Life Vision

My life vision describes in detail the way my life looks and feels when I am living authentically - as my full potential. It is the point on the horizon that defines the themes that focus my thoughts, behaviours and choices....

My life vision is:

My Work-Life Balance

Once I become more aware of who I am and what direction I am headed for the next chapter of my life, I can assess my work-life balance currently and identify where I want to focus my time and attention in order to achieve my life vision and live as my authentic self, more of the time ....

My work-life balance currently vs. optimally is:

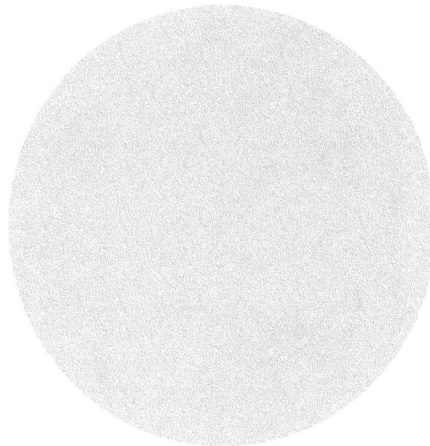

My Awakening

My awakening (wake-up call or aha) is what I am learning about myself from the personal clarity I am gaining.....

I am becoming awake to the following 3 things:

My Goals or Intentions

My goals move me forward toward my vision, are aligned with my authentic self, values and provide actionable steps I can take to live according to my leadership principles and purpose. I can also set more general intentions if it feels more comfortable for me....

The timeframe for my goals is:

My goals or intentions are:

Area of my life I would like to see improvement in:	Goal or intention plus one action I can take to move closer to achieving it:

My Inner Development Plan

My Inner Development Plan defines the focus for letting go of self-limiting beliefs by shifting how I think about my leadership as well as exercises for awareness and self-managing to be more effective....

The timeframe for my Inner Development Plan is:

My Inner Development Plan focuses on:

My goal:	
Limiting belief or behaviour and mindset shift required:	
Exercises to help shift or let go of it:	
Exercises for awareness and self-managing:	

My goal:	
Limiting belief or behaviour and mindset shift required:	
Exercises to help shift or let go of it:	
Exercises for awareness and self-managing:	

My goal:	
Limiting belief or behaviour and mindset shift required:	
Exercises to help shift or let go of it:	
Exercises for awareness and self-managing:	

My goal:	
Limiting belief or behaviour and mindset shift required:	
Exercises to help shift or let go of it:	
Exercises for awareness and self-managing:	

My goal:	
Limiting belief or behaviour and mindset shift required:	
Exercises to help shift or let go of it:	
Exercises for awareness and self-managing:	

My Community of Support

My support network is made up of people who provide me guidance, truthful insights and support as I continue my journey to leading and living as my best and authentic self....

My community includes the following supportive people:

Becoming "I"

Fear
Anger
Judgment

Out in the open now and exposed
for what they are....

Once seen and felt...
they dissipate - like clouds in the breeze move on and disappear.

Leaving the joy and light of awareness
the awareness that is "I"....

—Tana Heminsley,

Part Two –
Additional copies of the
Personal Learning Journal

Authentic You™ Personal Planning System
Personal Learning Journal

Date:_____

My Authentic Self

Knowing who I am when being my authentic self provides a glimpse of who I am when at my best – my potential....

When I am my best or authentic self I am:

My Values

My values define my core and most deeply held beliefs. They provide guidance for my thoughts, behaviours and decision making.....

I value:

My Purpose

My purpose clarifies what I am intended for in my life. It gives me meaning and defines the gifts I bring to others. It helps focus my choices....

My purpose is:

My Leadership Principles

My leadership principles translate my personal clarity about authentic self, values and purpose, into how I want each day to look....

My leadership principles:

My Life Vision

My life vision describes in detail the way my life looks and feels when I am living authentically - as my full potential. It is the point on the horizon that defines the themes that focus my thoughts, behaviours and choices....

My life vision is:

My Work-Life Balance

Once I become more aware of who I am and what direction I am headed for the next chapter of my life, I can assess my work-life balance currently and identify where I want to focus my time and attention in order to achieve my life vision and live as my authentic self, more of the time ....

My work-life balance currently vs. optimally is:

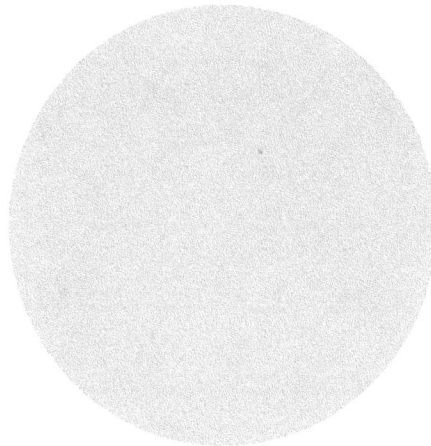

My Awakening

My awakening (wake-up call or aha) is what I am learning about myself from the personal clarity I am gaining.....

I am becoming awake to the following 3 things:

My Goals or Intentions

My goals move me forward toward my vision, are aligned with my authentic self, values and provide actionable steps I can take to live according to my leadership principles and purpose. I can also set more general intentions if it feels more comfortable for me....

The timeframe for my goals is:

My goals or intentions are:

Area of my life I would like to see improvement in:	Goal or intention plus one action I can take to move closer to achieving it:

My Inner Development Plan

My inner development plan defines the focus for letting go of self-limiting beliefs by shifting how I think about my leadership as well as exercises for awareness and self-managing to be more effective....

The timeframe for my inner development plan is:

My inner development plan focuses on:

My goal:	
Limiting belief or behaviour and mindset shift required:	
Exercises to help shift or let go of it:	
Exercises for awareness and self-managing:	

My goal:	
Limiting belief or behaviour and mindset shift required:	
Exercises to help shift or let go of it:	
Exercises for awareness and self-managing:	

My goal:	
Limiting belief or behaviour and mindset shift required:	
Exercises to help shift or let go of it:	
Exercises for awareness and self-managing:	

My goal:	
Limiting belief or behaviour and mindset shift required:	
Exercises to help shift or let go of it:	
Exercises for awareness and self-managing:	

My goal:	
Limiting belief or behaviour and mindset shift required:	
Exercises to help shift or let go of it:	
Exercises for awareness and self-managing:	

My Community of Support

My support network is made up of people who provide me guidance, truthful insights and support as I continue my journey to leading and living as my best and authentic self....

My community includes the following supportive people:

Authentic You™ Personal Planning System
Personal Learning Journal

Date:_____

My Authentic Self

Knowing who I am when being my authentic self provides a glimpse of who I am when at my best – my potential....

When I am my best or authentic self I am:

My Values

My values define my core and most deeply held beliefs. They provide guidance for my thoughts, behaviours and decision making....

I value:

My Purpose

My purpose clarifies what I am intended for in my life. It gives me meaning and defines the gifts I bring to others. It helps focus my choices....

My purpose is:

My Leadership Principles

My leadership principles translate my personal clarity about authentic self, values and purpose, into how I want each day to look....

My leadership principles:

My Life Vision

My life vision describes in detail the way my life looks and feels when I am living authentically - as my full potential. It is the point on the horizon that defines the themes that focus my thoughts, behaviours and choices....

My life vision is:

My Work-Life Balance

Once I become more aware of who I am and what direction I am headed for the next chapter of my life, I can assess my work-life balance currently and identify where I want to focus my time and attention in order to achieve my life vision and live as my authentic self, more of the time ....

My work-life balance currently vs. optimally is:

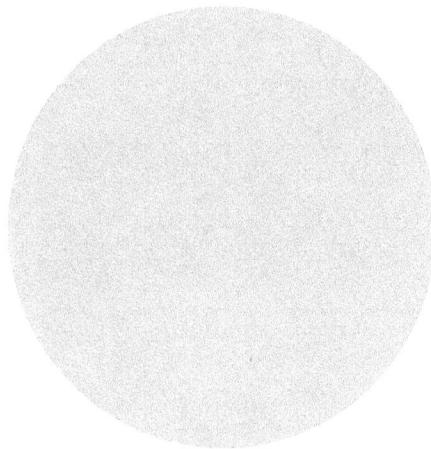

My Awakening

My awakening (wake-up call or aha) is what I am learning about myself from the personal clarity I am gaining....

I am becoming awake to the following 3 things:

My Goals or Intentions

My goals move me forward toward my vision, are aligned with my authentic self, values and provide actionable steps I can take to live according to my leadership principles and purpose. I can also set more general intentions if it feels more comfortable for me....

The timeframe for my goals is:

My goals or intentions are:

Area of my life I would like to see improvement in:	Goal or intention plus one action I can take to move closer to achieving it:

My Inner Development Plan

My inner development plan defines the focus for letting go of self-limiting beliefs by shifting how I think about my leadership as well as exercises for awareness and self-managing to be more effective....

The timeframe for my inner development plan is:

My inner development plan focuses on:

My goal:	
Limiting belief or behaviour and mindset shift required:	
Exercises to help shift or let go of it:	
Exercises for awareness and self-managing:	

My goal:	
Limiting belief or behaviour and mindset shift required:	
Exercises to help shift or let go of it:	
Exercises for awareness and self-managing:	

My goal:	
Limiting belief or behaviour and mindset shift required:	
Exercises to help shift or let go of it:	
Exercises for awareness and self-managing:	

My goal:	
Limiting belief or behaviour and mindset shift required:	
Exercises to help shift or let go of it:	
Exercises for awareness and self-managing:	

My goal:	
Limiting belief or behaviour and mindset shift required:	
Exercises to help shift or let go of it:	
Exercises for awareness and self-managing:	

My Community of Support

My support network is made up of people who provide me guidance, truthful insights and support as I continue my journey to leading and living as my best and authentic self....

My community includes the following supportive people:

Authentic You™ Personal Planning System
Personal Learning Journal

Date:_____

My Authentic Self

Knowing who I am when being my authentic self provides a glimpse of who I am when at my best – my potential....

When I am my best or authentic self I am:

My Values

My values define my core and most deeply held beliefs. They provide guidance for my thoughts, behaviours and decision making....

I value:

My Purpose

My purpose clarifies what I am intended for in my life. It gives me meaning and defines the gifts I bring to others. It helps focus my choices....

My purpose is:

My Leadership Principles

My leadership principles translate my personal clarity about authentic self, values and purpose, into how I want each day to look....

My leadership principles:

My Life Vision

My life vision describes in detail the way my life looks and feels when I am living authentically - as my full potential. It is the point on the horizon that defines the themes that focus my thoughts, behaviours and choices....

My life vision is:

My Work-Life Balance

Once I become more aware of who I am and what direction I am headed for the next chapter of my life, I can assess my work-life balance currently and identify where I want to focus my time and attention in order to achieve my life vision and live as my authentic self, more of the time ....

My work-life balance currently vs. optimally is:

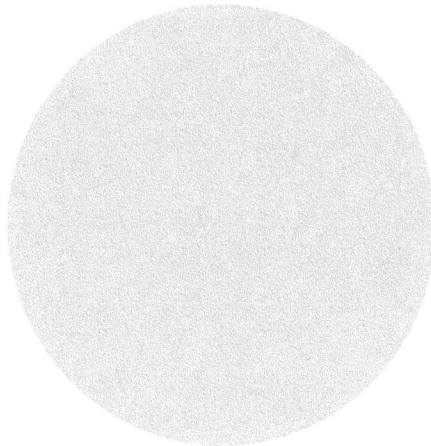

My Awakening

My awakening (wake-up call or aha) is what I am learning about myself from the personal clarity I am gaining.....

I am becoming awake to the following 3 things:

My Goals or Intentions

My goals move me forward toward my vision, are aligned with my authentic self, values and provide actionable steps I can take to live according to my leadership principles and purpose. I can also set more general intentions if it feels more comfortable for me....

The timeframe for my goals is:

My goals or intentions are:

Area of my life I would like to see improvement in:	Goal or intention plus one action I can take to move closer to achieving it:

My Inner Development Plan

My inner development plan defines the focus for letting go of self-limiting beliefs by shifting how I think about my leadership as well as exercises for awareness and self-managing to be more effective....

The timeframe for my inner development plan is:

My inner development plan focuses on:

My goal:	
Limiting belief or behaviour and mindset shift required:	
Exercises to help shift or let go of it:	
Exercises for awareness and self-managing:	

My goal:	
Limiting belief or behaviour and mindset shift required:	
Exercises to help shift or let go of it:	
Exercises for awareness and self-managing:	

My goal:	
Limiting belief or behaviour and mindset shift required:	
Exercises to help shift or let go of it:	
Exercises for awareness and self-managing:	

My goal:	
Limiting belief or behaviour and mindset shift required:	
Exercises to help shift or let go of it:	
Exercises for awareness and self-managing:	

My goal:	
Limiting belief or behaviour and mindset shift required:	
Exercises to help shift or let go of it:	
Exercises for awareness and self-managing:	

My Community of Support

My support network is made up of people who provide me guidance, truthful insights and support as I continue my journey to leading and living as my best and authentic self....

My community includes the following supportive people:

Authentic You™ Personal Planning System
Personal Learning Journal

Date:_____

My Authentic Self

Knowing who I am when being my authentic self provides a glimpse of who I am when at my best – my potential....

When I am my best or authentic self I am:

My Values

My values define my core and most deeply held beliefs. They provide guidance for my thoughts, behaviours and decision making....

I value:

My Purpose

My purpose clarifies what I am intended for in my life. It gives me meaning and defines the gifts I bring to others. It helps focus my choices....

My purpose is:

My Leadership Principles

My leadership principles translate my personal clarity about authentic self, values and purpose, into how I want each day to look....

My leadership principles:

My Life Vision

My life vision describes in detail the way my life looks and feels when I am living authentically - as my full potential. It is the point on the horizon that defines the themes that focus my thoughts, behaviours and choices....

My life vision is:

My Work-Life Balance

Once I become more aware of who I am and what direction I am headed for the next chapter of my life, I can assess my work-life balance currently and identify where I want to focus my time and attention in order to achieve my life vision and live as my authentic self, more of the time ....

My work-life balance currently vs. optimally is:

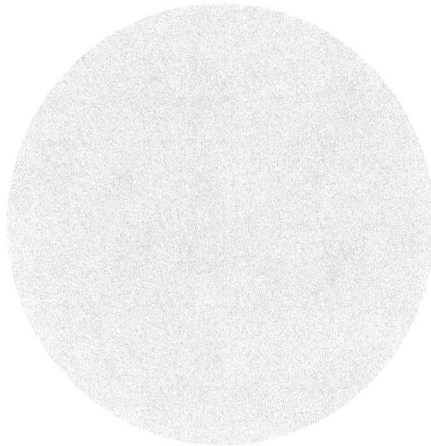

My Awakening

My awakening (wake-up call or aha) is what I am learning about myself from the personal clarity I am gaining....

I am becoming awake to the following 3 things:

My Goals or Intentions

My goals move me forward toward my vision, are aligned with my authentic self, values and provide actionable steps I can take to live according to my leadership principles and purpose. I can also set more general intentions if it feels more comfortable for me....

The timeframe for my goals is:

My goals or intentions are:

Area of my life I would like to see improvement in:	Goal or intention plus one action I can take to move closer to achieving it:

My Inner Development Plan

My inner development plan defines the focus for letting go of self-limiting beliefs by shifting how I think about my leadership as well as exercises for awareness and self-managing to be more effective....

The timeframe for my inner development plan is:

My inner development plan focuses on:

My goal:	
Limiting belief or behaviour and mindset shift required:	
Exercises to help shift or let go of it:	
Exercises for awareness and self-managing:	

My goal:	
Limiting belief or behaviour and mindset shift required:	
Exercises to help shift or let go of it:	
Exercises for awareness and self-managing:	

My goal:	
Limiting belief or behaviour and mindset shift required:	
Exercises to help shift or let go of it:	
Exercises for awareness and self-managing:	

My goal:	
Limiting belief or behaviour and mindset shift required:	
Exercises to help shift or let go of it:	
Exercises for awareness and self-managing:	

My goal:	
Limiting belief or behaviour and mindset shift required:	
Exercises to help shift or let go of it:	
Exercises for awareness and self-managing:	

My Community of Support

My support network is made up of people who provide me guidance, truthful insights and support as I continue my journey to leading and living as my best and authentic self....

My community includes the following supportive people:

The Light

There is only joy!

There is only love!

There is only peace!

I live as "I" wants
this is the possible life...

The new way...

For a new earth...

We are each the light

—Tana Heminsley,

What has Changed?

Each time you complete the Authentic You™ Personal Planning System, and recalibrate your Inner Guidance System, you will notice new things that you are learning about yourself. Use the following space to reflect on what is different since the last time, what has stayed consistent for you, and what the implications are for your next chapter. Also reflect on how you will celebrate the steps you have taken toward living as your Authentic or Best self, more of the time.

The date of the first time I completed the Personal Planning System:

The date of the second time I completed the Personal Planning System:

Reflections on what has changed since the first time:

The date of the third time I completed the Personal Planning System:

Reflections on what has changed since the second time:

WHAT HAS CHANGED?

The date of the fourth time I completed the Personal Planning System:

Reflections on what has changed since the third time:

The date of the fifth time I completed the Personal Planning System:

Reflections on what has changed since the fourth time:

Interview with the Author

What inspired you to write this companion workbook?

There are a couple of reasons why I wanted to write this book — first it took me many years to finally find where I fit in the world and to feel settled with a sense of personal contentment and meaning.

In addition, I have a passion for business, as well as a for leadership and personal development that I wanted a way to pair and share with others. And finally, I wanted a way to do my part — to help in the world, and I love to support leaders within organizations.

I have seen many people struggle either with trying to be themselves when they have been told they need to be something different in order to succeed. Or when they are impacted and find it difficult to live their true potential as their supervisors create negative conditions, they lose confidence and aren't sure how to move forward.

Over the years I have had the support of others and it has lead me to the understandings and experiences that are found in the book. So I thought I'd share them with others in the hopes that it will help them find where they fit, find meaning in what they do, and cultivate a way of being that is supportive for themselves, their teams and the world at large.

Who is the Authenticity Journal for?

This book can be used by both individual leaders, as well as organizational leaders (with their teams) and human resource professionals (with their internal clients and employees across an organization).

How can the Authenticity Journal be used in organizations?

The Authentic You™ Personal Planning System can be used in any number of ways within organizations.

First, it is flexible in it's delivery and customizable for different audiences.

I began sharing it with others as a 3-day retreat called "Realizing Your Full Potential". I then used it with coaching clients in 1:1 sessions, and to train others to deliver it for their clients. They then adapted it for different audiences – for women, for parents, for teens, for co-ed groups who wanted to live their "Authentic Roadtrips". We as a community realized it is useful for any person, anywhere at any time in their lives.

Second, it can be used for culture change and to support psychological safety.

At the same time as I was developing the Authentic You™ Personal Planning System, I had been developing both the process and topics for Authentic Leadership Conversations™. I realized that with the advent of social media that the art of conversation – real, rich, connecting conversation – was being lost. These facilitated conversations began to create safe havens where individuals could learn (sometimes for the first time) how to be authentic as they experienced it through the facilitator's way of being, and to begin a tactical practice of the foundational skills for authenticity themselves.

I also started sharing the Authentic Leadership Conversation™ process with women and men, with teams inside organizations and discovered that the Personal Planning system could be shared as a series of these conversations as a way for groups or teams to create deep bonds and trust while delving into their own personal work.

Third, the Authentic You™ Personal Planning System can be integrated into the talent and career development processes.

Imagine if every employee in your organization were to complete the personal exploration and transformative work to answer the big life questions that enrich their lives – Who am I at my best? What is deeply important to me? What am I meant to be doing with my life? How can I best contribute – to my family, organization, to the world? And then they would set goals or intentions for how to apply this very tactically to their work as well as to understand how self-limiting beliefs and behaviours may be getting in their way.

Imagine if they shared their insights with their peers, in facilitated, safe spaces where they could get to know each other more deeply than within the context of quick, superficial, daily interactions to get things done. The energy and connection that would occur would be palpable. Their relationships would deepen and the way they worked together for the benefits of Customers, Stakeholders and First Nations, would change for the better.

Imagine a meeting where everyone attending is unaware, uninterested in each other, and impatiently trying to get their point across so they can get to their next meeting. Now imagine that same meeting where each person has completed the Authentic You™ Personal Planning System and is aware of their thoughts and emotions, are practicing self-managing to override the unhelpful aspects of their ego or identity, and are practicing empathy and respect for the others in the room. The quality of the conversation would be richer and the outcomes would be better.

Which environment do you want to work in?

I know which one I prefer and that is why I have written these books and am sharing them with you now.

About the Author

Tana Heminsley is a thought leader, author, and integral coach with a focus on Authentic Leadership and Emotional Intelligence. In 2013 she published her first book *Awaken Your Authentic Leadership – Lead with Inner Clarity and Purpose.*

Tana is the recipient of the International Coach Federation Vancouver Chapter 2016 Coach Impact Award. This is the highest award category in British Columbia for coaching excellence for individual partnership (Coach Impact) level.

She is an executive and an entrepreneur with more than 30 years of experience building businesses and developing leaders.

During this time, Tana has been studying how individuals overcome childhood trauma to go on to become successful organizational leaders. She has researched extensively the inner journey of leaders and how it relates to long-term behavioral change and recovering from unhealed issues. When left unhealed, old traumas make themselves known as unhelpful behaviors that impact self and others (think the bully leader who grew up with an alcoholic parent who hasn't learned how to manage her/his anger).

She's a master at the practical application — the how — of emotional intelligence and authentic leadership. Both support leaders to heal old wounds and improve their effectiveness while experiencing more ease — in the workplace (and at home).

Her career has included roles such as:
- founding Authentic Leadership Global™ – an online-based business supporting organizations to transform their culture through individual and team growth and development.
- facilitating leadership development for 1000s of leaders through ViRTUS.
- being a member of the Executive team for BC Hydro – one of North America's leading providers of clean, renewable energy – with 4,500 employees, annual net income of $400 Million (2007) and 1.7 million customers.
- consulting for the founders of the balanced scorecard management system, which originated out of Harvard, and
- starting, owning and selling "Tana Lee" a retail clothing store.

Tana holds an Executive MBA from Simon Fraser University, Vancouver, B.C. Canada, a PCC credential with International Coach Federation, is an Integral Coach trained through New Ventures West, is a Certified Professional EQ Analyst, is a Certified Authentic Leadership Program Facilitator and has trained on the Enneagram.